Lester Westling, Vietnam-era chaplain and psychotherapist, reminds a nation conflicted by perspectives of war but united in concern for our service personnel and their families, how to honor them "When Johnny/Joanie Comes Marching Home." Direct and practical, Westling gives succinct historically-based and experiential background to the challenges of reuniting military people and families after duty-related absence, disruption, growth, and sometimes trauma. He then gives us a tested and proven program for both returning service members and for their spouses to prepare for current post-deployment family reunions—which can be duplicated and projected from the attached DVD for immediate use by leaders both abroad, at sea, and at home base.

By distinguishing between the honor and reverence bestowed upon World War II veterans versus the dismissal and betrayal Vietnam War veterans experienced upon homecoming, the author shows how the national populace's present support for their troops will result in greater healing for the nation as well as for those we send to war and families who anxiously await their return. Drawing upon his experience facilitating the reunions of these families during and after the Vietnam War, the author offers timely advice for returning service men and women, their spouses and children, and for all who care about them. Ordinary men and women face extraordinary demands and sacrifices when they deploy to defend us, as do those who remain at home in their support. Dr. Westling guides us into how to help such extraordinary people become whole families once again.

Ronald Mah, M.A.
California Licensed Marriage & Family Therapist
Instructor, Western Institute for Social Research

As a military husband and father who deployed and returned many times, the author's primary concern is for families who currently share these absences and reentries. From first-hand, front line experience, Les Westling has graciously written this book as a gift to every Commanding Officer, every Senior Enlisted Advisor, every Chaplain, every Ombudsman, and every Family Therapist concerned about the people entrusted to their care.

This is not just a theoretical discussion of the difficulties and dangers that come with the reunification of spouses and families following long separations.

The theoretical summary and discussion is very readable—however, this book is much, much more!

Les has included practical, tested tools for taking positive action to help spouses and families work through the difficulties and dangers inherent in homecomings from long deployments. Here are seminars, completely scripted, including the DVD movie clips necessary for their presentation.

This book needs to be part of every pre-deployment check-list and used as part of the planning for the end of every deployment.

Dave Carey, Captain, U.S. Navy (Ret.)
Author of "The Ways We Choose: Lessons for Life from a POW's Experience"
Motivational Speaker, Management Consultant, Coach and Trainer

Chaplain Westling has written a superb book on reuniting military family members after deployment. As a career Navy Chaplain with two combat tours in Vietnam, a licensed Marriage and Family Therapist who contributed to "Operation Homecoming" for the POWs from Hanoi, and who helped bring family therapy into the sea services—which later became the Family Service Centers—his insight into the importance of reuniting family members shows his professionalism, compassion, and concern.

Preparing for reunion by the deployed service member, as well as family members left behind in the homeland, is crucial for the success of sustaining longstanding, happy relationships, and even for retention in the military. Now, women who deploy in ships-of-the-line and as warriors in field combat, return to their own families. Their needs are new to the Armed Services, and are addressed by the Author.

As a veteran of 30 years with three combat tours in the Marine Corps, I have seen firsthand how crucial issues of return and reunion are. Chaplain Westling's book not only conveys the importance of understanding the dynamics of reuniting families separated by duty, but it offers excellent tools by which successful homecomings may be achieved.

Paul Siverson, Sergeant Major, USMC (Ret.)
Secretary, International Board of the Non-Commissioned Officers Assoc. of America
Member (2002-2004), Secretary of the Navy's Military Retiree Council
Member, Camp Lejeune Commanding General's Base Military Retiree Council

When Johnny/Joanie Comes Marching Home

REUNITING MILITARY FAMILIES
FOLLOWING DEPLOYMENT

The Reverend Dr. Lester L. Westling, Jr.
Chaplain, Captain, United States Navy (Ret.)

PRAXIS PRESS, INC.
GAINESVILLE, GA

When Johnny/Joanie Comes Marching Home:
Reuniting Military Families Following Deployment

Copyright 2005 by Lester Leon Westling, Jr.

ISBN 0-9754305-9-9
ISBN 978-0-9754305-9-0

Published by Praxis Press, Inc.
3630 Thompson Bridge Rd.
Suite 15-100
Gainesville, GA 30506
www.PraxisPress.com

Produced by Media Contractors, Inc.
www.mediacontractors.com

Cover: Navy Hospital Corpsman 3rd Class Michael D. Sarrazin (FMF) greets his newborn daughter Lily for the first time at the end of his 2005 deployment to Indonesia and Iraq with the 15th Marine Expeditionary Unit. His wife Susan is standing by.

All rights reserved.
No part of this book may be reproduced, stored in a retrieval system, or transmitted in any form or by any means, electronic, mechanical, photocopying, recording or otherwise, without the written permission of the author.

"We are all in the same boat in a stormy sea,
and we owe each other a terrible loyalty."
- G. K. Chesterton

Contents

ACKNOWLEDGMENTS IX

PREFACE XI

Part One:

CHAPTER 1: CHANGE HAPPENS 1
   Preparation – Forewarned is to be forearmed 3
   Keeping Bridges Intact and News Current 6
   Changes in Support Structures 8
   Deployment Conditioning 8

CHAPTER 2: THE COMBAT EXPERIENCE AND COMING HOME ... 13
   Indoctrination 13
   Bonding 14
   Surviving Combat 16
   Atrocities 19
   Rites of Purification 20
   Homecoming Adjustments 24

CHAPTER 3: IN SEARCH OF HOPE 31

CHAPTER 4: A LESSON FROM R & R 39
   Background 39
   Application 40

CHAPTER 5: THE REUNION 43
   Reentry Issues 43
   When *She* is the Returning Soldier 45
   Meeting of the Minds 48
   Mental Health Issues 49
   Best Friends 54

Part Two — Pre-Reunion Seminars

SECTION A: SEMINAR FOR RETURNING GROUPS 60

SECTION B: SEMINAR FOR SPOUSES 106

ABOUT THE DVD 118

ACKNOWLEDGMENTS

The motivation for writing this book has been solely for the purpose of making life better for military families who bear many burdens together for the defense of this country.

I have not been alone in this effort! My daughter, Karla Westling Bakke, M.A., of Glenwood, Maryland and my sister Harriet Westling Shank, M.M., of Seattle, Washington have professionally analyzed every page of the text as well as acting as proofreaders. Michael Wiley, M.S.W., of Whitmore, California, a retired Senior Chief Petty Officer and a fellow combat veteran of the Naval Riverine Forces in Viet Nam, has voluntarily traveled weekly to my office for 4-hour consultations about the text as it developed, and has contributed many thoughts and ideas. He has made many long-distance telephone calls, and has read and reviewed many references for this book. Michael has acted with persistence as Research Assistant, in order to document and verify many of the details that give this writing authenticity.

I would be remiss if I were not to mention the First Class and Chief Petty Officers of the former Human Resources Management Detachment, Alameda, California, who helped me establish in the Pacific Fleet the Pre-Reunion Family Seminars that are scripted in Part Two of this book. In rotation, one of them would accompany me from 1980 to 1983 to Pearl Harbor, where we boarded Battle Group ships returning from long deployments. We worked creatively as a team to present at least four Pre-Reunion Seminars for married and engaged personnel on each ship while underway for West Coast homeports. We transferred from ship to ship by helicopter, working long hours to accomplish our mission. Also to be commended are the chaplains and ombudsmen (who were spouses of sailors) who together presented the spouses' phase of these seminars at homeport in advance of the ships' arrival. I shall always be grateful for the professionalism and companionship of this remarkable group. When I was transferred to be Command Chaplain for USS *Carl Vinson* (CVN-70) and Battle Group *Charlie*, these seminars continued from 1983 to 1985 in its ships and aircraft squadrons. In this continuing endeavor, I was assisted by many talented military volunteers in the final weeks of our deployments. According to the Navy Chaplain Resource Branch, after I retired the Pre-Reunion Seminars were continued by chaplains in both the Atlantic and Pacific Fleets. It is with sincere regret that I cannot remember the names of each and every one of these leaders who shared with me a deep commitment to their fellow sailors, Marines, and their families.

This work has been an act of group devotion, and on behalf of all who contributed to this book and to the Pre-Reunion Seminars, it is our corporate hope that both will be found helpful for those to whom it is lovingly dedicated – our soldiers, sailors, Marines, airmen, and Coast Guardsmen, their spouses, and their children – all of whom are truly in the service of the United States of America.

PREFACE

When I was reunited with my family after each of two years in combat in Viet Nam, and even during one family reunion during Rest and Recreation (R&R) leave in Hawaii, I was confronted with adjustments that had to be made, and so were my family members. After my second Viet Nam tour of duty this led me to volunteer as a part-time participant at the Joint Center for Prisoner of War Studies in San Diego, preparing for the reunions of families in what would be named "Operation Homecoming." I then developed and executed a series of onboard pre-reunion seminars for married personnel returning in Battle Groups of Navy ships, and simultaneously for wives and relatives awaiting their returning sailors and Marines. Since then it has occurred to me that there are many civilian professions that require a parent to be absent for protracted periods of time: long-haul truckers, traveling salespersons, railroad workers, and some professional consultants, for example.

In the current configuration of the Armed Services, women deploy both to fleet and overseas unaccompanied tours as well as in combat. No longer do we address just the absent father in the experiences of these family separations, but wives and mothers as well. Some children team up with the remaining parent, but some experience rebellion motivated by anger resulting from the loss of a parent, even though such loss is temporary. Adults have more living experience that equips them to accept more easily the temporary nature and necessity of such separations.

Some family reunions following deployments and combat have positive outcomes. Absence can make the heart grow fonder. However, some families require years to adjust. Some reunions have resulted in domestic violence, even homicides. During my years as an active duty military chaplain I made many interventions to ward off the potential of unhappy occurrences. Lurid incidents made the news in 2002 when three rather senior soldiers at Fort Bragg, North Carolina, upon returning from Afghanistan, killed their wives. Some reunions never occur, because the spouse has left the home with the intent of divorce.

In this writing I have used such generic terms as service member, soldier, combatant, and returnee to describe the deploying family member. In addressing all of the uniformed services, such terms should be understood also to include sailors, Marines, and airmen of every rate, rank and gender, as appropriate.

The text of group programs for the enrichment of reunions of military families at the conclusion of deployment-separations is provided in Part Two of this book. The effectiveness of these programs was proven as they were conducted for over five years for all ranks and rates of married personnel in returning Pacific Fleet Battle Groups and for their awaiting spouses. This printing of the texts of the Seminars has been edited for multi-service use, and are suggested for use by Navy/Marine Corps Family Service Centers, Army Community Services, Chaplains, and military and civilian helping-professionals. Such programs for troops on the eve of their return might be conducted by mental health specialists deployed in the field, as in the case of the Army's Combat Stress Control Teams.[1] These Seminars were designed and are dedicated to making our military families members stronger and wiser as a result of the sacrifices they make to keep our nation both free and productive. Many splendid programs are now blossoming in support of the return and family reunions of the members of the various Armed Forces. Of special interest is the "Marriage Enrichment Seminar" series of the 101st Airborne Division conducted at Fort Campbell, Kentucky.[2] An 18-page publication entitled: *Return and Reunion Guide for Marines and Families* has been produced and distributed by Headquarters Marine Corps.[3] Of special value in this publication are a listing of adjustment needs of children of various age groups to the parent's return, and a section that addresses the single parent.[4] This booklet is available from Headquarters Marine Corps (M&RA), 3380 Russell Road, Quantico, VA 22134, and by telephone at 703-784-9012, and has been reproduced on the Internet at www.usmc-mccs.org, go to "Family Life," then "Family Separations."

A series of excellent booklets for various ages of children of deployed service members are available through the Marine Corps Key Volunteer Network, Camp Lejeune, NC, telephone 910-451-7550, or at MCAS, Cherry Point, NC, telephone 252-466-5779. They are as follows. An 8-page booklet which can be colored by a child is: "Your Parent Is Coming Home" (*A Scriptographic Booklet* by Channing L. Bete Co., Inc., One Community Place, South Deerfield, MA 01373; telephone: 800-628-7733 – request Booklet number 56820). "Let's Talk about Reunion" is an 8-page booklet for somewhat older children illustrated by a cartoon story, puzzles, and games (*Scriptographic Booklet* number 5683). "Deployment Days: A Coloring Calendar for Military Families" is a calendar with daily spaces for activities and with suggestions for parents during separations (*Scriptographic* item number 50443C-02-00). "Welcome Home! A Coloring Book on Military Reunion" is an 8-page booklet by *The Bureau for At-Risk Youth*, 135 Dupont Street, P.O. Box 760, Plainview, NY 11803-0760. "Preparing for Reunion" is a practical 8-page booklet full of useful ideas for adults (Channing Bete Company item number PS21378). This is also available though the "Key Volunteer Network."

When Johnny/Joanie Comes Marching Home is intended to enhance the services currently offered that support military family reunions. It offers additional background and guidance that may augment current programs or standardize future ones yet to be initiated. It is hoped that the insights suggested in this volume will bring enlightenment to families during necessary separations and in the reunions that follow.

Lester Leon Westling, Jr., M.A., D.Min., LMFT
Veterans' Day, November 11, 2005
At Redding, California, U.S.A.

---

[1] Phillip Thompson, "After the War: 'The Soldier's Heart' explores combat veterans' experiences," *Navy Times*, February 28, 2005: 30.

[2] Kimberly Hefling, "Army Tries to Save Marriages," *Associated Press* in (Redding, California) *Record Searchlight* (December 30, 2004): A-1, A-7.

[3] Personal and Family Readiness Division, Manpower and Reserve Affairs Department (M&RA), Headquarters Marine Corps, *Return and Reunion Guide for Marines and Families* (Quantico, VA, n.d.).

[4] Ibid., 13-15.

Part One

CHAPTER ONE

CHANGE HAPPENS

When we are parted from family members, friends, or even from our own hometown for a period of years, there is the expectation that everything will remain the same as it was when we were last together. Further, we are usually the last to accept the fact that we too change with time. Upon retirement, a colleague revisited the hometown he had not seen since he left to begin his career years before. He wrote a poem that ended with the phrase: "If you can't go home in the springtime, then never go home at all." Confronting change usually produces something of a culture shock.

This is no less true of one's experiences when returning from an extended period of unaccompanied duty. Although it is an exaggerated example when compared with the duration of most military deployments, many young married pilots who deployed to fly combat missions over North Viet Nam left marriage relationships in which they were dominant. Some wives reported that their husbands were used to even choosing their underwear, social activities, and the family diet before they were captured and imprisoned by the enemy. During the years of their prolonged absences, the wives of our Prisoners of War pioneered the Women's Liberation Movement without knowing it. Formerly subservient ladies organized to move the world to seek the release of their husbands. Wives who reluctantly took the initiative previously were pounding on congressional desks and making speeches in Washington, D.C. and in Europe about the needs of their husbands and their families. When their ex-prisoner husbands were finally released, the world observed through the media and their public appearances obvious changes in these men — both by the strengths and by the weaknesses they demonstrated. But many of them, in the privacy of their perceptions, became abruptly aware of the changes that had occurred in the personalities of their spouses. When a wife had found new and emboldened resources within herself, "this Genie would not return to her bottle" and needed to be valued for the new person she had become.

Many of the same dynamics that affected POW families may be present to some degree when the period of separation is the result of a shorter, more normal deployment. This is especially true when the spouse returns from combat or similar hazardous duties which yield uncertainties regarding the survival of the deployed one. A spouse with internal fortitude will become stronger during a deployment-separation. On the other hand, the spouse who is unprepared for the rigors of maintaining marital fidelity and executing family leadership alone during that time may be vulnerable, especially when not surrounded by one's own helpful family or the support of other mature military families. Army Community Services, Navy/Marine Corps Family Service Centers, or similar facilities, military chaplains or understanding faith groups can be helpful, if the spouse will turn to them. The Navy Ombudsman program has proven itself to be a most valuable safety net or supplement for awaiting spouses when other positive support is not present or summoned.

Preparation – Forewarned is to be forearmed
A well-planned and well-prepared marriage is the basic foundation for any family building. But this is especially true where the stresses and concerns of military life and duties will be involved. The ups and downs of married life are given realities. In order to strengthen the vows "for better for worse, for richer for poorer, in sickness and in health, to love and to cherish, until parted by death," premarital counseling before the marriage is optimal. This may be available for the couple conjointly or in groups (such as Pre-Cana or Engaged Encounter), and these are the best sources of strength for future military couples.

All too often, however, the Recruit will rush home after boot camp to marry the high school sweetheart, with little foresight as to what is to follow. Weddings swamp the calendars at Academy Chapels and at Officer Candidate Schools immediately after graduations. The rush into marriage following school completion, on the way to one's first duty station, carries stresses when the new priorities of the services may take precedence over building strong interpersonal foundations. At the time of this writing, reserves are being mobilized, National Guard units are being activated, and the Navy and the Air Force are exercising "surge" plans which make Battle Groups and Wings subject to sudden deployments. In a recent *Navy Times* article entitled "Rushing Down the Aisle," Karen Jowers makes reference to Fort Polk, Louisiana; San Diego County, California; and both Fayetteville and Cumberland County in North Carolina as military concentrations that are experiencing a surge of marriages.[1] "'When deployments occur, we absolutely see a significant increase (in marriage licenses),' said Gregory J. Smith, county clerk and commissioner of marriages for San Diego County, Calif.… According to Defense Department statistics, more than 15 percent of active duty troops deploying in 2003 and 2004 got married within a year of their deployment." Experienced military couples have the potential for handling deployment separations more maturely, but age does not necessarily condition in positive ways.

One of the best means of preparing for deployments and reunions that follow is the strengthening of the initial marriage bond in realistic ways, and the resulting foundation for family building. In Recruit Training Centers and in Officer Training Commands, premarital group counseling for those intending marriage, conducted by chaplains, military social workers, or through the Family Service Centers, is most worthy of committed time in training schedules. For several years when I was one of the staff chaplains at Naval Training Center, San Diego, I conducted evening marriage preparation groups for Recruits, so I know that this can be done. Although this flies in opposition to the age-old adage that if the military wanted you to have a wife or family, they would have been issued to you, such counseling possibilities reinforce the military family as a team to endure moves, deployment separations, and post-deployment reunions. Indeed, the positive effect on the retention and dedication of skilled personnel will be obvious, and well justifies such programs.

Sound financial management is a must for mutual understanding and teamwork in a new military marriage. Planning for separation periods can ward off marriage-threatening difficulties. Lonely people face the temptation to overspend, be it in the malls at home base, or at the vendors or bars in exotic lands and ports overseas. For the service member, buying lavish presents to be sent home or saved for the reunion might be an attempt to overcome guilt feelings for being away from loved ones. For the lonely spouse, self-sorrow can also be temporarily assuaged by unplanned spending which can get out of control. Overseas telephone calling is subject to escalating costs in a competitive market in spite of the oversight of the Federal Communications Commission. The length and frequency of this important link need to be rationed intelligently.

Spouse and parent meetings just before deployments are routine in most military units, and many include important information. Some are presented in creative ways with handout materials and the introduction of family support resources that are vital to families separated by military duty. However, some such meetings are conducted in perfunctory ways that fail to inspire retention of the information provided.

I was Command Chaplain of the carrier *USS Carl Vinson* on her first cruise. Sailing around the world from the shipyard and Norfolk to our first homeport of Alameda, California necessitated a move across country for most families of the crew. During that cruise my office responded to over 4,000 Red Cross emergency messages in a period of nine months. The next deployment was of similar length and with a similar complement of 6,500 crew and air wing on board, but it was easier to gather people to prepare them for this, because the cross-country moves already had taken place for most. The Ombudsman Program, composed of mature wives that had been trained, was in place throughout the counties surrounding homeport. (All Ombudsmen were *wives* because there were no women in the crew at that time.) During the final phase of that second cruise, I held pre-reunion seminars on board the carrier and ships of the Battle Group in advance of arrival, with simultaneous seminars held by professionals at homeport to prepare the spouses for the return of their husbands. (See Part Two, Sections A and B respectively for the content of these seminars.) Only 1,000 American Red Cross emergency messages to the ship were received and responded to on this cruise. There was a dramatic decrease in Emergency Leaves during the deployment, and domestic crises were substantially reduced after arrival of the ship. This demonstrated the positive effect of programs that are designed to prepare military families to greet each other at deployment's end.

Keeping Bridges Intact and News Current

Keeping both spouses current during separations minimizes adjustments and surprises to be encountered upon homecoming. This is now much easier in most situations. E-mail through computer availability in many land locations and on board ships has been a most welcome addition to telephone and regular mail services, all of which are great positive morale factors. On the other hand, some duties require staying in remote places or being on combat patrols where no or very limited communications are available. The service member needs to explain this to the spouse in ways that will not compromise a classified mission. An understanding of this situation at home can be essential to the peace of mind of all concerned. Correspondence builds bridges across miles of lands and seas, and therefore has the potential for keeping relationships dynamic during the inevitable growth experiences that occur while families are apart.

It is good to place numbers on letters that are exchanged in both directions, so that if they are received out of order, the disturbance in sequence will not lead to misunderstandings. When there is only routine about what to write, then one can write about the routine. Especially for the deployed member, home routine will be received as vital and he/she will feel included. A walk in the park with a child, flowers that are growing in the window box, school activities and grades, or what is happening on the job are never perceived as boring when coming from a loving spouse, father, or mother. Should the days of either party seem all alike, it is possible to divide one's day into a sequence of parts, each of which might provide interesting material for a number of letters. The solution is not as simple for the deployed service member who may have to guide around classified information or combat actions. However, this is a challenge rather than an excuse not to correspond.

It is also possible to use a multimedia approach. From a remote location or in advance of departure, the absent parent can tape-record bedtime stories to be played for children at home. The human voice provides reassurance of security. Photographs are important, yet with the understanding that icons do not scold or discipline – a concept which will have to change when the absent parent returns.

Only a familiar voice beats the handwritten letter. It is important for the deployed parent to write letters or address tapes separately to each member of the immediate family – especially to each child. Effort is recommended to tell each one a unique story or incident tailored to the interest of the recipient. Military duties have their times of demanding action, but these are tempered with times of boredom as well. Field missions alternate with times in the rear. Where there is a will, a way can be found.

Overseas telephones are now available in some forward locations. In addition to electronic mail, satellite telephones are a growing option for overseas communications. These are important adjuncts to Red Cross emergency messages in times of need. There is a natural tendency to protect the deployed parent by withholding negative reports. However, the sharing of family news is important, so that the absent parent will not feel excluded from life at home. For the reporting of most crises that do not demand the presence of the service member, it is good to convey the information to the service member – *but to tell of the matter following a resolution, or at least a partial resolution, when possible.* For example, "Johnny broke his arm on the park swings, but Dr. Smith set it and put on a cast, and he only missed a day of school." Or, another: "My car was hit in the parking lot last week, but the other guy's insurance will cover it, and the car will be fixed by the dealer by next Friday."

Changes in Support Structures

During the time apart, especially when the deployment period has been very stressful for either or both parties, unanticipated changes occur in the sources of support for the family. Likewise, there may occur changes in the attitudes of either or both parties in regard to such personal resources. These support structures may include the neighborhood, the job of the at-home spouse, political party, the stock market, or even the military itself. Nothing remains static even when we are focused elsewhere.

Relatives or important friends may have moved in or out of the geographic area or of a helpful relationship position.

For some, the faith group and spiritual resources are major matters of personal concern. The service member may be caught by surprise on return by changes in the policies or traditions of denomination, temple, or mosque unreported during the absence. Experiences while deployed may have increased faith, or may have alienated one or the other of the couple from previous beliefs.

Such matters are essential topics for the exchange of information during deployment, or upon reunion at the conclusion of the time away.

Deployment Conditioning

The term "conditioning" means that the experiences we have influence changes in our thinking and ways of doing things. During prolonged periods of separation, it is hard to see changes that occur in ourselves, and as stated before, it is difficult or impossible to imagine how conditioning has caused changes in those removed from our daily associations.

Imagine the environment surrounding spouses separated by deployments. The military member is immersed in a disciplined and demanding structure. Decision-making and precision are required, and there is the expectation of punctuality. He/she becomes used to the receiving and giving of forceful orders. Even shorter separations such as temporary (additional) duty assignments (TDY or TAD) are easier for the traveler busy with new distractions and away from the home routine and responsibilities. On the other hand, loneliness for family can become intense at times. Commonly the service member hopes for uninterrupted quiet time at home with spouse and children upon his/her return.

For the spouse who has remained at home, there is the responsibility of setting the pace alone for home and family. There may be children, or employment, or both, with which to contend. Strong resolves to handle the juggling act according to the expectations of the couple often erode with time and tiredness of doing it all alone, and growing youngsters are known to respond to the "single" parent by cleverly testing limits and finding means to get their own way. Being alone and limited conscientiously to the house and to child raising restricts one's social life. When baby-talk is the primary means of communication, the lack of intellectual stimulation can weigh heavily on the parent. If the parent lives in base housing, there are others with whom to share and with whom to find understanding, and military childcare facilities and recreational activities are available. If the parent is near her/his home and family of origin, there may be similar opportunities for support. But for the military family situated in the civilian community and without a supportive faith group or other means of fellowship, during the absence of the other parent, this military spouse may feel marooned, and become overly anxious.

For the spouse/parent committed to home and family during the deployment of the other spouse/parent, there is the growing hope that upon reunion there will be an escape from this confinement. A growing yearning for opportunities for some outings, travel, romance, and happy excitement can be expected, and will need satisfying at deployment's end. Negotiation with a returnee who covets hearth and home over the selection of shared outside activities may reduce stress in the reunion.

For the children this couple may have, the absence of one parent may seem hard at first, but later a matter to which adjustment has become routine. Children sense the attitudes of the parent to whom they are so close during this period, and they tend to reflect the internal content or anxiety of this parent and act it out in their behavior. Children's behavior is often a clue to the true feelings of the parent, even if not outwardly confessed.

The oldest child (or another) may have been unwittingly welcomed by the parent as the "Man (or Woman) of the House," responding to real needs for help and babysitting during the deployment. However, this "surrogate parent" may be set up for a disappointment when the service member returns to rival that status, unless family members are given to understand the process in advance. In this period of renewed patriotism in America, the deployed parent may be envisioned over the extended period to be as he or she appears in photographs – a hero or heroine to be admired. This expectation can complicate that image when the deployed parent returns and takes part in parenting responsibilities and helping with the stability of the family structure.

As children grow during the period of absence of one parent, they rapidly advance through important stages in their young lives, each child with expectations of his own. These stages involve their education, social life, and physical development – all of which are intensely important to them and to their understanding of themselves. Likewise, parenting expectations will have changed during the 6 to 18 months of deployment. The absent parent will not find the emotional landscape of the family unchanged upon return. Opening himself/herself to learning from and listening to the other spouse is crucial, and demonstrates the importance of correspondence during the separation. It may even be advantageous to seek the help of a professional family therapist upon return. Therapy would require an adjustment for the deployed one who is used to being "the person in charge." Likewise, the previously homebound parent needs to accept the help and strength of the returnee, especially if the one providing leadership alone at home has grown tired and the discipline has worn thin during the separation. Mutual acceptance of aid upon return requires a great deal of trust and privacy during the reunion adjustment period. But it is a positive opportunity for the parenting couple to listen and learn from each other. When the subject of discussion is setting limits and disciplining the children, this is best done out of the hearing of the children.

Change happens in the lives of military couples and in their offspring. It happens during the absence of the service member, and it needs to be assimilated with understanding by all family members upon the reunion of the family. Change is a constant factor in military life, with moves, orders to new posts or commands, new schools and communities. Change can be harsh. But the challenge is to harness change so that it works in favor of all concerned, rather than fighting its losses with lasting sorrows over what must be left behind. *Change* can be seen as a friend, with opportunities for growth. Encounters with change can build the military family into a team that accepts the hardships as well as the joys. Such is the great challenge for every military family.

---

1. Karen Jowers, "Rushing down the Aisle," *Navy Times*, January 10, 2005: 47-48.

CHAPTER TWO

THE COMBAT EXPERIENCE AND COMING HOME

Many fine books on the subject of combat have been written by tacticians, psychologists, and combat veterans. This writing is not intended as a comprehensive treatment of the subject. However, this particular chapter is offered with a focus on what might have transpired before a combat veteran returns, that it might be helpful specifically to the family welcoming him/her home. Not every deployment involves combat or direct encounters with an armed aggressor, and this entire book is intended to be helpful to a more inclusive readership. This specialized chapter is dedicated to returnees from battlefields or the air above them, and to their families.

Indoctrination

Boot Camp begins a process that must be continued in such facilities as Infantry Training Regiments or in close air support training at such facilities as Fort Rucker, Alabama. The social mandate to kill even in close encounters must be indoctrinated into military personnel who have been sent by the nation for war-fighting. By way of example, in the case of a firing squad tasked to execute by higher authority, the squad is composed of a number of marksmen. This way, the "killer" (the fatal bullet and the exact shooter who fired it) can never be precisely identified. This provides psychic protection for the shooters.

Lieutenant Colonel Dave Grossman, throughout his book *On Killing: The Psychological Cost of Learning to Kill in War and Society*, stresses that the dictates of social conscience common to humankind have strict injunctions prohibiting killing within the species.[1] It is important that there be a differentiation between the soldier and the criminal in the mind of the society that mandates the killing, and especially in the mind of the warrior himself. Grossman makes the point that for the trainee to overcome this great conflict in order to kill in battle (including in law enforcement), especially when one can see the enemy, training must include repetition of practice conflicts with targets in human form.[2] This conflict in the soldier (who is not the rare psychopath) becomes more intense the closer the enemy is perceived to be, both in physical proximity and in cultural identity. Defamation of the enemy as a subspecies eases the combatant's ability to kill him or her.[3] It is easier for artillery and bomber personnel to accomplish their lethal missions from a distance than it is for the foot soldier or for those providing very close air support. In addition, Wayne Smith reported on surveys of our combatants in the *Navy Times*: "14 percent of soldiers and 28 percent of Marines reported that they 'experienced being responsible for the death of a non-combatant.'"[4] This has also been a part of many nightmares that plague soldiers after battles, evidence that wars cannot erase the community of humankind.

Bonding

Seasoned military leaders recognize that the primary source of motivation for the warrior is feeling an intense responsibility for the protection of one's comrades. Grossman states: "This bonding (between comrades-in-arms) is so intense that it is the fear of failing these comrades that preoccupied most combatants."[5] This fear of failing colleagues in combat rules out the fear of death or mutilation as the *major* inhibiting factor for the modern soldier. However, my observations in combat revealed that the older the soldier, the greater the apparent anxiety for personal safety and recognition of the value of one's own life and continuing responsibilities. Fulfilling the expectations of one's superiors also ranks high on the list of motivations for the professional soldier.

To demonstrate that the importance of bonding in soldiering is not a new discovery, the following quotation is offered from William Shakespeare's *The Life of King Henry V*. King Henry (in the disguise of a soldier) encourages his "fellow warriors" thusly:

> *We few, we happy few, we band of brothers;*
> *For he today that sheds his blood with me*
> *Shall be my brother; be he ne'er so vile,*
> *This day shall gentle his condition:*
> *And gentlemen in England now a-bed*
> *Shall think themselves now accursed they were not here,*
> *And hold their manhoods cheap whiles any speaks*
> *That fought with us upon Saint Crispin's Day.*[6]

This bonding among warriors is indeed a huge factor, because it is apparent in post-combat grieving of combat survivors. Trauma intensifies the bond between those who experience it together, whatever the source of the trauma. Indeed, the heat of combat forges immutable comradeship. Sir William Fraser wrote prophetic words: "The battle of Waterloo was won on the playing fields of Eton."[7] Teamwork and leadership are considered primary to one's survival in armed combat. It was well known in Viet Nam that any outfit that did not clean up after an encampment and fill in their fighting holes before moving on was undisciplined, and these units were followed and engaged because the enemy considered them to be easy marks.

The challenge upon coming home from war is to apply this team commitment to spouse and family as well. While not forgetting fellow veterans, bonding with them need not rival dedication to the "home team" which demonstrated their support and faithfulness throughout prolonged absence, with all the uncertainties of having their service member in remote and hazardous duty.

Surviving Combat

> *"Cannon to right of them, Cannon to left of them,*
> *Cannon in front of them Volleyed and thundered;*
> *Stormed at with shot and shell, Boldly they rode and well,*
> *Into the jaws of death, Into the mouth of hell Rode the six hundred."*
> ~ Alfred Lord Tennyson [8]

To survive under fire, one must act instinctively to every threat and every perception of intrusion. When one is confronted by encroachment, survival requires instantaneous reactions. There is no time to think about anything else, nor can one surrender to one's feelings—no matter how powerful they are. Combat requires emotions to be buried—perhaps for revival at another time and place, perhaps not. This conditions the combatant, over time, to repress feelings. After I was on operations in the field and under attack, suppressed emotions would catch up to me "in the rear" where there was relative safety. Nightmares and vomiting became expected after-action visitors. This taught me that one's body cannot long be denied by the discipline of one's mind.

Yet, soldiers who have practiced such denial through a number of encounters can develop a talent for burying unwelcome thoughts and feelings. Bad memories can thereby be blocked, at first voluntarily, but this can develop through practice into an involuntary practice of hiding them in the unconscious. From that vantage, they can intrude at unexpected times when either sleeping or awake. The inability to come to terms with feelings can serve not only to block bad memories, but also to isolate the former combatant from those around him or her. The ability to know one's emotions *at the instant that an event or encounter is happening* is a gift, the restoration of which may require the time and talents of a professional psychotherapist when the returnee is in a position to seek such assistance.

A combat soldier is most vulnerable at two times: on first arrival, and just prior to leaving the contested area. When units are mobilized together, all enter and leave the combat zone at the same time. But when individuals are deployed as replacements, the "new guy" is not only conflicted by inexperience, but may lack the confidence of his comrades. Just prior to leaving the hostile area, troopers can be tired or overly confident, thus becoming careless. Leaders need to be alert to such individual needs, even when they are ignored or denied by the soldier.

Killing is a very uncomfortable thing to contemplate, especially as a duty that must be performed. New arrivals will confront overwhelming resistance to killing in combat. But after a number of encounters, such as firefights in which he or she is charged with the rush of adrenaline, the soldier will be emboldened to hurdle fear in order to respond defensibly. A motion picture about airborne soldiers in Viet Nam was called *The Deer Hunter*.[9] Although the film is fiction and does not connect this similarity, the title suggests that for the experienced sports hunter and the seasoned infantryman there are parallel motivations—such as, the exhilaration of the kill and the commitment to the hunt. This realization helps us understand some of those who have been in combat, even though not every combat veteran admits to the same emotional response. The combatant can even become unjustifiably and irrationally "intoxicated" by the excited condition of killing, to the point of welcoming future battle challenges. Dave Grossman quotes the term "Combat Addiction," to describe this phenomenon.[10] The progression of conditioning to combat is like dealing with the familiar experience of "buck fever" for the hunter, according to Grossman, or to "stage fright" for the performer, with its adrenaline surge or rush.[11] Such experiences can only be managed if the energy is harnessed through training, rather than overwhelming its "victim"—in this case the rifleman. Throughout his book, Lt. Colonel Grossman emphasized that the presence and influence of leadership in the field, revenge for the loss of comrades, and the intense need to protect one's fellows, are important ingredients that expedite the soldier's functioning in combat.[12] As a chaplain with Marine Infantry and with Naval Riverine Forces in combat, I was not technically a combatant. However, I was there and able to observe the importance of these factors in battle situations. Jonathan Shay, M.D., Ph.D., writes: "War itself always creates situations in which physical survival contradicts moral survival."[13]

Unlike most movies and television dramas, combat does not involve constant and continuous times of frenzy. Operations do involve frightful encounters. For infantry, exhausting marches for days and nights in succession are routinely required, as well as digging a new fighting hole each dusk, often without drinking water and basic hygiene. Urban warfare involves house-to-house searches for the enemy. Both types of operations always subject the soldier to the tension of confronting an ambush or surprise encounter. Supply convoys in Southwest Asia (the Middle East) require similar prolonged alert postures in expectation of explosions or attacks. In close air support, opposition is always expected, and aviators experience the same adrenaline rushes and alertness as do the ground-pounders. But there are also times in the rear, bivouacked between operations, which are occupied with the cleaning of weapons and with administrative duties. Such times can be boring as well as restful. One is always on alert in contested areas, especially when the danger of being overrun, of incoming mortars or artillery, or of a terror attack persists. The constant reliance on being alert takes its toll on a person, and is destined to have a residual effect on the soldier, even when he/she is rotated to a safer position.

Atrocities

Yes, atrocities happen. Some come to light in the media or by government confession. The most prominent in Viet Nam was My Lai; the most prominent so far in Iraq has been Abu Ghraib Prison. When a soldier sees his friends killed or mutilated in the fury of battle, or when anger is generated for other reasons, emotions can exceed rational restraints. Wrath can escalate exponentially in the human psyche, and tragedies can result that violate the strategies of war. In the excitement of battle, there are those who lose track of basic human ethics. Senior on-site leadership is essential for the prevention of atrocities, because peers may not dare to intervene or report such incidents.

As a chaplain for two years in Viet Nam combat, I saw little of this aberration of conduct – some possibly having been prevented by my presence in the field. I stopped several minor incidents, and was instrumental in having a Company Commander relieved for rewarding unacceptable behavior by his troops against the enemy. Dr. Shay writes: "Vietnam narratives reveal that the events that drive soldiers berserk are betrayal, insult, or humiliation by a leader; death of a friend-in-arms; being wounded; being overrun, surrounded, or trapped; seeing dead comrades who have been mutilated by the enemy; and unexpected deliverance from certain death."[14] He continues concerning the self-perceptions of the one who has lost control in combat: "Whether the berserker is beneath humanity as an animal, above it as a god, or both, he is cut off from all the human community when he is in this state."[15] Dave Grossman writes: "Those who engage in a policy of atrocity usually strike a bargain that exchanges their future for a brief gain in the present ...Our own post-World War II studies showed that in England and in Germany little was accomplished by (the strategic bombing of cities) except to steel the resolve of the enemy."[16] Indeed, atrocities deny the humanity of the perpetrator(s) and energize the opponent, and thus are self-defeating rebellious tragedies.

Rites of Purification

Because killing is contrary to the human conscience, there will always be guilt associated with war – both for the soldiers and for the tribe or nation that dispatched these humans to the fight. Because of this, intense indoctrination is necessary to ensure that troops will actually fire their weapons at the enemy.[17] Likewise, there needs to be an exit strategy that will expedite the return of combat veterans to society. For it to be effective, this exit strategy must address both the returning soldiers and those whose mandate sent them into battle.

Sir James George Frazer, in his revolutionary 1922 anthropological volume, *The Golden Bough*, has provided a comprehensive description of *rites of purification* observed for returning warriors and huntsmen by African, Asian and American aboriginal tribes.[18] These rites include the isolation of the returnee until a form of ablution by washing or smearing can be performed. The primary motivation for these animistic rituals reportedly is for the propitiation of the spirit of the slain enemy (or beast, in the case of the hunter), ensuring that its spirit would not return to harm the warrior. According to Frazer, the reason for isolating the warrior from the tribe until after the ritual of cleansing was a common belief that this was necessary to protect the tribe, as well, from the retribution of the spirits of the dead. Thus, in ritualistic behaviors observed by anthropologist Frazer, many similar practices were held among tribes distant from one another on many islands and continents. These rituals were intended for the magical protection of both the warrior and the tribe that dispatched him to war. Jonathan Shay identifies these disciplines as having been observed by the Hebrew Tribes under Moses and Eleazar.[19] Animistic tribes still exist in remote places today. When serving as a missionary in the Cordilleras Mountains of Luzon in 1960, I lived in close proximity to animistic pagan barrios, and visited them frequently.

Lieutenant Colonel Grossman refers us to Arthur T. Hadley, a multi-decorated veteran of World War II, and author of the book *Straw Giant*. Grossman writes: "Hadley (also) conducted an extensive study on major warrior societies around the world. In this study he concluded that *all* warrior societies, tribes, and nations incorporate some form of purification ritual for their returning soldiers, and this ritual appears to be essential to the health of both the returning warrior and the society as a whole."[20]

Anthropological research reveals that rites of purification for combatants returning from battle were administered as an ablution or washing, often cleansing not only the body of the warrior, but also his clothing, fighting implements, and armor. With many similarities to the Sacrament of Christian Baptism, this quasi-religious ceremony is said to have the intent of forgiveness—absolving the returning warrior of the guilt of war, and permitting reentry into community. This absolution rite also involves the tribe or state which administers the rite—*because it mandated the actions of those whom they sent to war*. Dr. Shay states: "The ancient Greeks had a distinctive therapy of purification, healing, and reintegration that was undertaken as a whole community. We know it as the Athenian theater."[21] Here the warriors' stories were told, sung, and reenacted. Some of these have come down to us in the heroic folk ballads of Greek epic poetry, in the dramas of Homer, and the trilogies of Aeschylus.

Irrespective of rites of purification reputed to have existed in antiquity and in remote tribes, those returning from deadly combat in our time require absolution, and the society that dispatched them needs to own responsibility for the killing it ordered, as they welcome their soldiers back into society. This provides assurance that the actions in battle, so foreign to human injunctions, are not offenses, but are rather valued and claimed by the parent population.

Returnees from the battles of World War I and World War II were greeted by parades, cheering crowds, commendations, and decorations that were recognized beyond the boundaries of the military. These modern purification rites expressed the doctrine that these soldiers had acted under the mandate of their nation, and that they were regarded as heroes who had not acted on their own. These wars were considered *holy wars* by Americans and the Allies, in which "our soldiers" had protected the American homeland by keeping the killing and the destruction overseas. These warriors reentered society as "the Greatest Generation," proud ever since, because "we were in it together!" Those who went to these wars returned truly devoid of lingering guilt because the tribe, our nation, claimed responsibility for these wars, and for any war-related guilt identified with these violent conflicts. Our warriors were seemingly absolved. Horrible memories seemed cleansed.

Some frontline troops in the Korean conflict (which veterans call "The Forgotten War") harbored second thoughts about their mission, but many veterans who questioned the conduct of that war kept their feelings of anger and regret to themselves upon return home. Veterans of the war in Viet Nam were also denied purification rites by their nation (and by their neighbors), when they returned. Therefore, they—and, vicariously, some of their family members—thanklessly carried upon themselves the war-related guilt of the nation, as well as their private recollections of battles and bereavements. This guilt would remain unresolved for years – if not forever. The pain they experienced when they returned from war was, in good measure, inflicted by the very population that sent them. Many found limited comfort by attending reunions of their former units, and for those who accepted help, from the clinicians of the Department of Veterans Affairs (VA).

In his second book about Viet Nam veterans, *Odysseus in America*, Jonathan Shay makes this appeal: "As a society we have found ourselves unable to offer purification to those who do the terrible acts of war on our behalf. I believe this is something to be done jointly by people from all religions, from the arts, from the mental health professions, and from the ranks of combat veterans – not from the government. What I have in mind is a communal ritual with religious force that recognizes that *everyone* who has shed blood, no matter how blamelessly, is in need of purification."[22]

The nation has belatedly learned much from the Viet Nam War and its veterans. Many changes are evident in troop handling in current conflicts in Southwest Asia, and in the expressions of support from the American citizenry. Currently, the nation is offering rites of purification plentifully to veterans of Iraq and Afghanistan, and to their families. Veterans of previous conflicts are now vicariously receiving the benefits of a renewed patriotism. The September 11, 2001 attacks on our homeland demonstrated the value of our military serving in distant conflicts overseas, which has protected our neighborhoods from the holocausts of war. Regarding this war, more citizens are supportive of our troops even if they do not agree with the decisions that sent them to Afghanistan or Iraq. Surely our troops will return from current conflicts to a wiser nation, military, and citizenry.

Homecoming Adjustments

Some things are helpful for the self-assessment of the combat veteran upon his return, as well as for the understanding of his family to whom he returns. Living and fighting in conditions dictated by war over a prolonged period will change a person. Thus, there are important factors which will help in understanding the returnee.

The intensity of the combat experience is inversely proportional to the distance between the combatant and his enemy throughout his tour of duty. That is, the closer the soldier has been to the enemy, the greater the stress inflicted upon that soldier. There is an exception: in guerilla warfare, the degree of closeness to one's enemy is always a matter of doubt, which contributes to the tension endured. (This is a strategy valued by terrorists.) However, if the returnee was "in the rear with the gear," in a relatively secure position for the deployment (as essential as every duty assignment is), he/she will present differently in homecoming than one who was consistently on the frontlines or in convoys through contested areas. In his book *Up Front*, Bill Mauldin warns: "Look at an infantryman's eyes and you can tell how much war he has seen. Look at his actions in a bar and listen to his talk and you can also tell how much he has seen. If he is cocky and troublesome, and talks about how many battles he's fought and how much blood he has spilled, and if he goes around looking for a fight and depending on his uniform to get him extra-special privileges, then he has not had (the combat experience)."[23]

Another matter deserves consideration. In past wars, and more often in the conflicts in Southwest Asia, military personnel have been transported to and from theaters of war in groups as a unit. This is helpful to the soldier, and the current emphasis on preserving unit integrity probably is the result of lessons learned from Viet Nam. The predominant mode of transport from the overseas wars previous to the 1960s was slow and arduous. Military Transports were ships rather than airplanes, and homeward voyages took weeks rather than hours. All these factors worked in favor of the personnel, because they had time with their comrades to debrief one another before they were surrounded by family (and perhaps by the media). Slow voyages with access to comrades relieved a great deal of pressure. This allowed the returnee to be more thoughtful in the selection of what might be revealed and shared with his/her dependents, friends, and the world beyond.

Eighteen hours after I was airlifted from Firebase Con Thien in the Viet Nam Demilitarized Zone under heavy artillery fire, I was standing on the tarmac at Travis Air Force Base in California, greeting my wife and young daughter. This was after a year of absence with all of the uncertainties of war. None of us on the chartered home-bound airplane knew each other, because we were all from different units, even different military services. The only thing we had in common was our jungle green uniforms. Within the large passenger cabin during the long flight home there was silence, as each soldier was obviously deep in his own thoughts. Troops usually went to Viet Nam as individual replacements. When their time was done or they were critically injured, they were extracted individually from their units and sent home, dispersed with permanent change-of-station orders or a discharge. Although no one complained about being carried out of the war zone promptly, there were no opportunities for informal discussions and reassurances among those who had shared so much. Buddies were rarely located after returning from the war. Combat veterans arrived home, as I did, with their heads spinning with unresolved issues, making it difficult to give their full attention to awaiting loved ones who were eager to offer love and attention to their "returning hero."

By the time of the Viet Nam War, the United States had developed the most efficient methods of managing the logistics of war. But the most "efficient" method of managing *the major instruments of warfare* — the people who must go and fight — has proven to be an emotional disaster. Currently, returnees from Afghanistan and Iraq have the luxury of a swift return by flight, which robs them of the time needed to adjust to anticipated new surroundings and family reunions. But one cannot put pages back on the calendar. This is the age of rapid travel, and we would not have it otherwise. However, as has been lauded above, now it is more common for soldiers to go to war as a unit, and also to return with their buddies. Casual debriefings are routine among military friends who understand each other, and who speak a common language about common experiences—if they can find each other. This may continue as their units regroup in the homeland, at reunion gatherings, and/or in individual encounters. It is important for the families of combat veterans to honor the need for such opportunities for communication in the ongoing life of their returnee, and not feel excluded by this need.

Sharing with buddies is safe, but only a first step in communality. The family is a necessary second step to the veteran's reintegration into society. It is equally important for spouses and relatives to demonstrate that they are interested in hearing the stories of their combat veteran when he/she is willing to share them. This is the very threshold by which the combat veteran can reenter the larger community beyond the military. This requires the spouse and relatives to exercise active listening skills, and to have the fortitude to hear what needs to be shared (and perhaps excuse an occasional slip in vocabulary). Listening is a means of expressing honor.

The memory of violence remains prominent in the human psyche, and it can replay itself involuntarily with intrusive conscious episodes and in nightmares. This is frequently compounded by true or imagined survivor guilt over one's performance in past crises. "Did I do enough? Could I have saved the others?" Even without justification, such doubts haunt many survivors, and this phenomenon is a common aftermath in most grieving—whether it is for the loss of a friend in war, or the loss of a loved one in times of peace. But if such thoughts are not quelled, they can provoke the need to revisit a horrifying memory. In the extreme, such doubts can provoke the self-doubter to retest his/her behavior by needlessly attempting renewed hazardous challenges—such as driving too fast, or attempting other unnecessary feats of daring and danger.

Much is being researched and written about the psychological wounds of war. In this tide of developing concern, the visible wounds of war that attract immediate sympathy may need continuing emotional and physical assistance throughout the remaining lifetimes of the veteran and his/her family. Scarring, amputations, paralysis, or blinding are disabilities that remain far beyond the initial medal ceremonies and reunions, and these will impact the abilities of the returnee and change his/her role in the family. Becoming suddenly dependent on others for basic living skills has a tremendous effect on both the returnee and the adjustments required of family members. The self esteem of the disabled veteran is threatened by a negative potential for future employment, and even by limited abilities to perform some jobs around the house that once were expected as a matter of routine. Of the many fine existing veterans' organizations with potential for helping and that have volunteer Service Officers at military hospitals and Department of Veterans Affairs (VA) facilities, the Military Order of the Purple Heart and the Disabled American Veterans have as their primary objective assisting fellow wounded veterans in recovery even beyond hospitalization, and local chapters can be easily located.

On April 30, 2004, the U.S. Army created the Disabled Soldier Support System (DS3) for those veterans with disabilities 30 percent or greater. "The program is designed to provide advocacy for soldiers for five years as they recuperate and prepare to return to or leave the service."[24] The Marine Corps is developing a similar program to provide assistance to injured Marines and their families.

The Army's DS3 office can be reached at 800-833-6622 or on the Web at *www.ArmyDS3.org.*

In spite of the therapeutic efforts and benefits provided by the VA and the military, the disabled veteran and the family will daily, even hourly, bear the burdens of the wounds of war. This challenges family members of the disabled veteran to accept a unique teamwork, demonstrate courage, and recognize that they are quietly sharing the heroism that war and its residuals require.

It must be emphasized that most who return from war are handling their lives well and productively, even courageously. Cataloguing prominent achievers and effective leaders whose direction and energy came to life after the experiences of combat is quite possible, but beyond the scope of this writing. In short, the residuals of combat experiences are not all bad. On the other hand, *People Magazine* reports, "a recent Army study found 15 to 17 percent of veterans from the current Iraq war are suffering PTSD (Posttraumatic Stress Disorder)—roughly the same proportion as Vietnam vets."[25] So, when preoccupied with violent memories and/or survivor guilt; when the combat veteran's tolerance for frustration seems alarmingly low; when it seems that the returnee is struggling with his/her emotions, is constantly alert or startled, or is isolating him/herself from society, these bold clues indicate that professional therapeutic intervention is needed. The *macho* culture of the military delays many returnees from seeking therapeutic help for post-traumatic stress. But when such symptoms as described are evident, the earlier adequate care is accepted, the sooner peace of mind for both the service member and his/her family may be anticipated.

The combat veteran commonly returns home physically and emotionally exhausted, filled with memories, grieving lost friends, and entertaining secret doubts of his/her past performance. I can testify to this, having "been there and done that." Following a rapid return "to the world," many such thoughts are congested in one's mind. Everyone who returns from combat needs to be heard, even though not everyone is ready or willing to share. As stated before, to listen is to honor. All who return from combat need to be honored. This is our current rite of purification. This can be the very portal to coming home.

I close this chapter about the combat experience with the final comment that when one is in a crazy situation, feeling crazy may be a healthy adjustment to the surrounding reality. But when one has returned to the safety of one's homeland and family, the compassion and understanding of others is the ablution and absolution that heals and helps one leave the war behind, so that new and unnecessary conflicts may not be created – be they imagined or real. Thus, it is possible that a well-deserved peace may be found and enjoyed by all involved. To listen is to honor.

---

1. Dave Grossman, *On Killing: The Psychological Cost of Learning to Kill in War and Society* (New York: Back Bay Books - Little Brown and Company, 1996), 29-39.
2. Ibid., 107-10, 131-33, 156-173.
3. Ibid., 92-93.
4. Wayne Smith, "For the Troops on the Ground, Iraq Might As Well Be Viet Nam," *Navy Times*, September 27, 2004: 54.
5. Grossman, *On Killing*, 90.
6. William Shakespeare, *The Life of King Henry V*, Act IV, Scene 3, Lines 60-67.
7. William Fraser, *Words on (Arthur Wellesley, Duke of) Wellington* (1899).
8. Alfred Tennyson, *The Charge of the Light Brigade* (1854).
9. Michael Cimino, Deric Washburn, Louis Garfinkle, Quinn Redeker, *The Deer Hunter* (Universal Studios, 1978).
10. Grossman, *On Killing*, 244-45.
11. Ibid., 29, 231.
12. Ibid., 144, 179, and passim.
13. Jonathan Shay, *Achilles in Vietnam: Combat Trauma and the Undoing of Character* (New York: Scribner, 1994), 197.
14. Ibid., 80.

15. Ibid., 86.
16. Grossman, *On Killing*, 206-8.
17. Ibid., 22-27.
18. James George Frazer, *The Golden Bough* (New York: The Macmillan Company, 6th abridged edition, 1958), 246-52.
19. Jonathan Shay, *Odysseus in America: Combat Trauma and the Trials of Homecoming* (New York: Scribner, 2002), 152-53; with reference to *Numbers* 31:19-21.
20. Grossman, *On Killing*, 271-72; with reference to Arthur T. Hadley, *Straw Giant* (New York: Avon, 1987).
21. Shay, *Achilles*, Note 14, 230.
22. Shay, *Odysseus*, 245.
23. Bill Mauldin, *Up Front* (New York: W. W. Norton and Company, 2000), 42-43.
24. Karen Jowers, "DS3 at Their Side: Fledgling Army program cuts red tape to help war wounded," *Navy Times* (November 22, 2004), 24. The DS3 was renamed on November 10, 2005 as the "U.S. Army Wounded Warrior Program."
25. Richard Jerome, Andrea Billups, Susan Keating, and Joanna Blonska, "Bringing the War Home," *People* 62, no. 24 (December 13, 2004), 98.

CHAPTER THREE

IN SEARCH OF HOPE

"Thus says the Lord... 'Remember not the former things, nor consider the things of old. Behold, I am doing a new thing; now it springs forth, do you not perceive it? I will make a way in the wilderness and rivers in the desert.'"
~ *Isaiah 43:16a, 19-20*

The Matson luxury liners had been converted hastily into troop transports at the outset of World War II. Previously they had carried 722 tourists to Hawaii and the South Pacific. After conversion, each of them carried over 5,000 troops to the theaters of battle. When hostilities had ceased and the ships were candidates for restoration, it was found that the teak deck rails had been carved with the names and initials of soldiers facing battle. In an obvious attempt to be remembered, many had left their mark in this fashion. Whether to leave the rails as they were or to replace them was a matter of controversy for their owners.

Yes, "Kilroy was here" (a popular slogan of that war), and "Kilroy" wanted to be remembered, whether he lived or died. This is a demonstration in the midst of war of the human search for hope. This search is one all humans share "in the best of times and in the worst of times." This search for hope in the midst of threats from a world in conflict is what we love about the indomitable GIs that have defended our nation throughout its history. It is the plea of the soldier who would much rather be going on civic action operations than operating his lethal weapon.

In Viet Nam, infantry battalions held "County Fairs," calling people out of their villages to a place where medical, dental, and various welfare contributions could be made, while other Marines searched vacated huts for stashed weapons and hidden entrances to escape tunnels. The troops favored opportunities to provide assistance to indigenous people. American youth is at its best when confronted with a humanitarian challenge. Response of our military to the tsunami disasters in Asia in December 2004 and in U.S. Gulf Coast States in late August and September 2005 challenged our service personnel to give their typically unselfish best. Civic action is the "plum," the most cherished opportunity even for voluntary service, for our military personnel. This is a giant factor to be taken into account either abroad or at home.

When I was chaplain in USS *Carl Vinson* (CVN-70), I would recruit volunteers to help with reconstruction projects in orphanages or hospitals in foreign ports. When 50 were needed, 400 would volunteer; when 85 were needed, 600 would ask to join. When the war is over for older and disabled veterans, many attend unit reunions and participate locally in veterans' organizations, where they actively seek ways to be helpful to others.

We can only imagine the power for persistence emanating from the mental image of that girlfriend, wife, parent, or child of the sailor on a ship in the Persian Gulf, in the mind of the soldier on the DMZ in Korea; of a Marine in Fallujah, Iraq, or an airman flying out of isolated bases or off a carrier deck. These who are so remembered amidst hazardous and lonely duties and long and weary hours of work, are anchors in that search for hope in the middle of challenges for survival and resistance to temptations. Families at home need to be aware of their importance to their service member on duty. Special days are observed as happy milestones amidst the deployment environment. Such important dates as birthdays, anniversaries, and family reunions are remembered. I can still recall how important survival was for me in the midst of one terrible battle. My thoughts were on my son who was 9 months old that night, and I wanted to see him once again. Such is the search for hope that keeps one going.

One remarkable quality in American culture is the presence of optimism in the midst of the impossible. Americans will instinctively make a joke out of an obstacle that seems unchangeable. Soldier Bill Mauldin kept morale alive during the darkest days of World War II in Europe with his cartoons of two soldiers of his invention, Willie and Joe. They spoke their minds (and the otherwise unexpressed thoughts of typical enlisted personnel) in the midst of blood, mud, and exhaustion. His book, *Up Front*, a collection of many of his drawings with his commentary about them, was destined to become a best seller for all time.[1]

Funny things do happen, even in combat, for those who can see them as funny, and who understand their importance during hard times. Observers may call it "gallows humor," but on the contrary, humor is indispensable in the search for hope. Infantry Marines taught me to keep my heart up and my head down. Common slogans exchanged on search and destroy operations were: "Another grand and glorious opportunity to excel; one good deal after another!" "Every day's a holiday, every meal's a banquet!" While on the receiving end of a heavy artillery bombardment, my chaplain's clerk yelled to me from his fighting hole: "Chaplain, it's good for your career!"

None among us in the combat zone failed to see the humor even in borderline events that happened. At an underground firebase (where latrines were the only thing on the surface), a Marine artilleryman told me that he had been hit in the head. I responded that his head looked all right to me. He said: "No, Chaplain. I was sitting on it!"

When a wounded Marine was being examined in the triage of a field medical battalion, the surgeon was offended by the mess in his trousers that were being cut off to reveal his wounds. The fearful young man responded, "But Sir, we was ambushed!" The attending medics exploded with laughter, and never allowed that physician to forget it.

A soldier with the Army Engineers was building a bunker when his ladder collapsed. As he jumped to safety, he swallowed a tenpenny nail that had been held between his teeth. The triage physician, who was inundated with casualties that night, shouted out his orders: "Feed that man lots of bread, X-ray daily, and report the results. Next case!" The rapidly working staff was amused, but returned to the business at hand. Three days later there was a "plink" from below him in the outhouse; we cheered, and the soldier was returned to duty.

The battalion hospital corpsman set up at dusk too near a tree. While he was enjoying his C-rations, incoming mortar fire drove us all into our holes. When he called out that he had been hit, we crawled to his rescue in the dark. It was soon discovered that what felt like a wound to his posterior was a prick from a shard of glass from his exploded Tabasco sauce bottle, and what to him felt like his blood was the contents of the bottle that had been hit by shrapnel.

These are just examples of events that may not have been found amusing under other circumstances, but in worrisome times they took their rightful place in search of hope.

What surprised me the most in serving as a military chaplain was the openness and spontaneous search for faith that I observed among service members. By comparison, when I have served as a pastor in the civilian sector, I have had to expend more energy to interest people of this age group. The adage that "there are no atheists in foxholes" has a high percentage of truth, but this also applies to the wider audiences of those whose military duties and deployments routinely do not involve combat. Military personnel lead disciplined lives if they wish to succeed, but this requires them to think for themselves in this century in which the services aggressively utilize advanced technology. Therefore, there is greater stress on education and self-improvement. Indeed, it is "up or out" in the promotion strategies of the present armed forces. Our modern military values and retains persons with initiative as never before. Thinking people seek meaning in their lives, and in their pursuits as well. I found this reflected in the pursuit of a meaningful religious faith in the search for hope and meaning among individual service members.

Religious services during deployments at sea and in the field, whether led by an ordained chaplain or by a lay leader, seem to be attended by a higher percentage of the population than of those who worship in the civilian sector. During my tour in the aircraft carrier USS *Carl Vinson*, 35 religious events each week were conducted on board by chaplains and by trained volunteer lay leaders, with Sunday morning Protestant and Roman Catholic services held in the covered forecastle attended by 200 worshippers per service. Weekly chapel gatherings included those for Pentecostal Christians, Latter Day Saints, as well as Jewish and Islamic personnel. Lay leaders in the smaller ships of the battle group held regular Sunday services, augmented by chaplains when the "Holy Helo" could get chaplains to them in rotation. Once a month, Jewish personnel were picked up from surrounding vessels on Friday afternoon by the "Hebrew Helo" for Sabbath services and a kosher evening meal on the carrier, returning them to their commands the next morning. These worshippers augmented the weekly Jewish services on board the carrier. Even though long periods at sea make worship/study opportunities "the only show in town," the level of response to opportunities to participate in chapel-related activities demonstrates an eager constituency.

Years ago, when a service member came to me as a chaplain seeking to affiliate with a faith group, I would routinely be correct when asking: "What's *her* name?" However, more recently I have found those who are asking questions about religious faith are sincerely struggling to remember their Sunday School lessons, Bible instructions, or catechism lessons gained in their younger years. Many are thoughtfully searching with a new concern and enthusiasm. During deployments at sea and in the field, at the request of young service persons, I have baptized in the canals of Viet Nam, in a hotel swimming pool in Abidjan, Ivory Coast, in empty halves of aircraft engine shipping containers on the carrier hangar deck at sea, in the surf at a beach on Guam, and where an inverted ship's bell was used as the font.

Although it may be an extreme example, one of our prisoners of war who returned from Hanoi told of how he occupied time and energy recording Bible phrases and portions of the *Book of Common Prayer* that he could recall. He used charcoal from a warming fire to write on saved toilet paper. His endeavors were typical of his fellows during their captivity.

Pastors are always delightfully surprised when a sermon or a service they have provided has been remembered. I have received reports that lessons have been retained and utilized even years later by some military persons who had attended brief religious services conducted when deployed in the field. Three stories that follow illustrate the level of commitment among such personnel.

During my time, Marines called each other "Animal," probably because we had to live like animals, we smelled like animals, and we had to fight like animals. On Easter Day 1967, a service of Holy Communion for a company of 1st Battalion, 4th Marine Regiment was being held on the beach at the mouth of the Cua Viet River in Viet Nam. The service was interrupted by incoming mortar rounds during the sermon. As the troops scattered, I yelled after them: "The meaning of Easter is that we are *not* animals!" The implication was that we are not to behave or to think like animals. Years later, I met Marines that were in that gathering who understood and remembered the message.

In late afternoon on May 21, 1967, the day following a fierce battle to gain Hill 22, I gathered a group in a corner of the battlefield surrounded by jungle still smoldering from napalm and close air support. At Evening Prayer, I reminded the troops of how we learned in a class at Camp Pendleton to recognize "night noises." I reminded these Marines to stay alert for an approaching enemy, yet also to keep in mind, as they spent the night guarding the perimeter, that they would hear sounds of the wind in the trees, and birds singing or in flight. I asked that they not lose sight of the fact that not everything beyond them was hostile – that the peace we were defending beyond the war was a reality – and it was this hope that awaited them. My congregation understood this, and I was given reports months later that this brief homily was influential in the lives of troopers as they prepared to return home.

On May 18, 1970, in the Mekong River at a place 21.5 miles into Cambodia called Neak Luong, the five or six Viet Nam Navy LSTs our "Tango" riverboats had escorted partway toward Phnom Penh came back down the river. They had been dispatched to rescue Chinese and Vietnamese residents that were being slaughtered in an effort of ethnic cleansing by the Communist government. These ships were loaded to the gunwales with their human cargo, which was estimated at 100,000. It was *at the request of the sailors* that we drew our boats together in the Mekong for a brief Eucharistic service of thanksgiving for the successful rescue, before continuing downstream to the Viet Nam border and to relative safety.

Rethinking religious faith, wishing to be remembered, thinking of loved ones at home, finding humor amidst chaos, striving to be helpful and to do meaningful things—all these stand as self-generated aids to succeeding in the face of difficult situations that can be encountered in military life and duty. These are all-important steps in the search for hope during deployment. Recognition of such learned skills in the life of one returning from a prolonged separation will, in good measure, be an aid to discovering new strengths in the life of the service member. Appreciation of these facets in the returnee will be assets to honoring his/her return, and the application of such skills can make a great difference to the military family following deployment.

---

1. Mauldin, *Up Front,* passim.

CHAPTER FOUR

A LESSON FROM R&R

Background

Grieving is the process of letting go or the reframing of something or someone that has been treasured. One may be grieving the loss of a person, a limb, or possessions, but for our purposes here the focus is on the loss of a relationship by death or the presumption of death.

The symptoms of grief were first defined by Erich Lindemann in 1951.[1] Elisabeth Kubler-Ross in 1972 identified in simplified terms various emotional and behavioral stages that are somewhat predictable in grieving, which she described as a prolonged journey from denial, through anger, to acceptance.[2] In his 1958 book, Edgar N. Jackson called this process of letting go *grief work*.[3]

In their 1971 recorded observations of caregivers of terminal patients at the University of Minnesota Center for Death Education and Research, Robert and Julia Fulton coined the phrase "Anticipatory Grief Work."[4] They identified irreversible grief work that was acting in the lives of those attending to the terminally ill *in anticipation of their deaths*. The closer the relationship to the one preparing to die, the more intense was the grief work experienced by their caregiver. When the death occurred, there was an unexplained feeling of relief that seemed inappropriate and inconsistent with the expectations of the caregivers and their observers. Yet the researchers concluded that the grief work had been done in anticipation of the death, and that *this was irreversible.*

In my doctoral research and dissertation, I proposed that for wives who had concluded (consciously or unconsciously) that their husbands were never going to return alive, anticipatory grief work was involuntarily acting on them.[5] If this process was not interrupted early enough, the process could be irreversible. In short, (in the case of my study) even if their POW returned alive, the returnee's survival would not be emotionally acceptable to one who had subconsciously buried him. Obviously, great changes occurred in the lives of these couples and families during the seven or eight years they were apart. But it is suggested that anticipatory grief work, rather than sheer disloyalty or infidelity on the part of the spouse, may have been a covert factor in many of the divorces that followed "Operation Homecoming."

Application

The Rest and Recreation (R&R) program, implemented during the Viet Nam War, reunited many combat troopers temporarily with their wives and even family members for a brief week's vacation in a safe location. A similar program has been reactivated for spouses separated by the conflicts in Southwest Asia, in many cases bringing the soldier home for a visit. Therefore, a lesson from the first R&R program may have relevance to the current conflict.

It is suggested that a service member on R&R with his/her spouse, who needs to do some sharing, may relate graphic details of what his/her combat duties entail and harrowing episodes that may have been experienced. Such revelations halfway or more through the deployment may startle the spouse with the probability that the service member might not return alive, thus initiating a process of anticipatory grief work. If not interrupted after the couple bids goodbye and the loved one returns to the front, given time, this *anticipatory grief work* could become irreversible in the ruminations of the spouse. Similarly frightening information might also be conveyed through e-mails or letters, but it is more convincing when it occurs during a face-to-face encounter on a mid-tour visit on R&R or at home. Having survived the remainder of the tour of duty, the combatant may not find love awaiting him/her on return. This can happen by surprise without either party understanding the phenomenon.

Interruption of anticipatory grief work can be accomplished by a friend or a therapist. It can be opened by a simple and frank inquiry, such as: "Do you think he may not come home alive?" Few have the fortitude to venture such a question, but this brings what might be an overwhelming worry to consciousness, where it can be discussed. Real fear can be triggered by information shared by the loved one on hazardous duty, and will not be quelled by a "Not to worry, Honey; everything's going to be all right" response. But when the fear has surfaced, its control may be broken, and the concern can then be defused by realistic yet rational discussion(s) with an understanding respondent.

A careful and empathetic listener might make a therapeutic intervention that could interrupt fear generated anticipatory grief work, thereby saving a loving bond upon which a marriage has been built.

---

1. Erich Lindemann, "Symptomatology and Management of Acute Grief," *Journal of Pastoral Care* V (Fall 1951): 19-31. Reprinted from *American Journal of Psychiatry* CI (September 1944).
2. Elisabeth Kubler-Ross, *On Death and Dying* (New York: The Macmillan Company, 1972).
3. Edgar N. Jackson, *Understanding Grief, Its Roots, Dynamics and Treatment* (New York and Nashville: Abingdon Press, 1958), 15-43.
4. Robert Fulton and Julie Fulton, "A Psychosocial Aspect of Terminal Care:

Anticipatory Grief," *Omega* II (May 1971): 91-100.

5. Lester L. Westling, Jr., *Manual for Ministry to Prisoner of War Returnees and their Families in the Long-Term Readjustment Period* (unpublished doctoral dissertation at San Francisco Theological Seminary, San Anselmo, California, and Naval Postgraduate School, Monterey, California, 1974).

CHAPTER FIVE

THE REUNION

Reentry Issues

"The second thing I want to do when I see my wife again is take my hat off!" said the Marine Sergeant in anticipation of the connubial reunion. No question was posed as to whether or not the waiting partner might have the same thoughts.

In a Spouse Support Group during a deployment time, I heard a wife express her inability to put her relationship completely back together immediately upon her husband's return, without time and consideration of the changes both of them undoubtedly experienced during the separation. She said: "I can't go to bed with a stranger." She demanded an opportunity for mutual recognition of the new people both had become.

When I was invited to the table for my first meal at home after thirteen months away, it was suddenly discovered that the normal places had been set, but a setting for me was lacking. Naturally this was quickly resolved and embarrassment was expressed. But these true tales demonstrate that the need for adjustments may exist for both the returning service member and the home folks.

Bachelor living and duties with one's deploying unit—be it at sea or on foreign shores—creates a "second family" (that has been called a "band of brothers/sisters") with unique bonding that adds to the accumulation of experiences, expectations, and friendships of the one who has returned from deployment. Likewise, the spouse may have spent the separation time in college, on a job, or rearing children and keeping house, each domain having its new colleagues, associates, and responsibilities. New friends and new experiences need to be shared, and ideally this would be a time for a honeymoon-like retreat for the purpose of catching up with one another. Finances, change-of-station orders, and the presence of eager children may present obstacles to such private times for intimacies and debriefings, but it is important for such opportunities to be high on the list of priorities.

As a deployment draws to a close, frequently (as a chaplain), I have been asked: "What should I confess to my spouse?" The choice is always left to the inquirer. However, with the risk that my readers may find this answer controversial, my advice has been as follows. First I ask if debt or physical disease or anything that will involve the corporate life of the couple has been contracted. Without a doubt, such matters must be shared, and the partner appealed to for help. Beyond that, I ask: "Who will benefit from such a disclosure?" If a confession to the spouse is simply to make the penitent person feel better but may yield great distress to the partner while resolving nothing, I advise that this possibility be taken into consideration. I then have left the choice to the one inquiring.

A spouse who has been eagerly anticipating the return of the partner for renewal of affection and to share the responsibilities of home and family may be looking for some relief, and for time away from the confinement that such duties require of one facing them virtually alone. On the other hand, the returnee may be expecting undisturbed time at home – with travel and excitement left behind. These desires need to be discussed and negotiated soon in the post-deployment reunion.

Childcare and discipline is another matter that needs to be discussed. The one at home may be tired of scolding and guiding. Both child control and household repairs may have become relaxed due to tiredness in maintaining such endeavors alone. The returnee, as has been previously stated, may find that the family environment does not stand up to "military expectations." When children are involved, there is the mutual need for both parents to assist one another. The waiting spouse can help the returnee reacquire the closeness and attention to the needs of their children after the separation, and to relax duty-related discipline. Likewise, the returnee can help with the structure and the control of their children and give attention to needed home and car repairs. A deploying single parent who has relied on grandparents or other parent-surrogates to be custodians of the children and keep up with other necessities during the absence may find him/herself torn between gratitude for this effort and feeling expectations have been compromised.

When *She* is the Returning Soldier

Her hometown newspaper interviewed Melissa Wanty, a 23-year-old soldier, when she was on two-week home leave after duty in Tikrit, Iraq.[1] The report states: "Her reality is far from keg-parties, all-night gab-fests with her girlfriends, or working a 9 to 5 job. Wanty is trained to kill, identify land mines, and drive a five-ton vehicle across dangerous territory. She's not trained to ask questions." Likewise, the single woman soldier who would not likely be satisfied to join her civilian peers in activities common to them, might feel more isolated at home than when on duty. When a female soldier returns to husband, perhaps to children, her own adjustments and the adjustments of her hosts upon return would focus far more on her dependents than upon her family of origin and her neighborhood. This could be easier, because her own family would have shared daily in the necessary sacrifices to support her service, and would have the potential of being more understanding than others might be.

The female service member reuniting with loved ones and a surrounding community may be returning from deployment serving in an aircraft carrier, overseas in a military hospital, an Air Force squadron, a support base, a patrol boat, or from combat. However, for her, the impact will be different from that of her male counterpart—as different as emotional life differs for different genders.

Women entering formerly all-male worlds have unfairly had to be change-agents in a system in which designated leaders do not always understand, monitor, or enforce. Frequently this has cost the pioneers great pain. Men have had to learn that women can carry their own tools and "man" their own weapons. At the same time, the perception of intrusion into what was formerly exclusively "a man's world" has been resisted by covert demonstrations of prejudice. Fortunately for women in the military, observant authorities have been swift in the attempt to provide a level field, and good superiors have been able to mold their troops into a positive team, thus reducing endangerment in the pursuit of a common mission. But women in the military services are not strangers to the struggle described. Rarely, a woman unnecessarily feels compelled to match the unsavory actions and language commonplace among "the boys" in order to fit in, rather than keeping her own values (whatever they may be), thereby failing to define gender equality on a professional basis.

In 1984, off the coast of Kenya, I boarded USS *Prairie* (AD-15), one of the first ships to integrate women into the crew. I asked the Commanding Officer (CO) of this destroyer tender how it was going. He replied that the women were competitive in their skills, indeed proving themselves and their abilities, and that they provided a generally calming effect upon his crew. I inquired if he had been able to keep sexual problems at bay in this young coeducational crew. He responded that a schedule of fines for fraternization administered at Captain's Mast (CO's hearing with penalties awarded) kept relationships on a professional basis. Specifically, holding hands would be cited at $100 a hand; kissing at $150 a lip, and beyond that he left to my imagination. The initial introduction of females into deploying crews sparked some concern among wives at home, but news of structured command leadership has been reassuring to spouses.

This background is offered because it undoubtedly influences the dynamics of post-deployment reunions for female military personnel with family members and friends. Truly, temptations and jealousies are bound to occur in a military in which both genders comprise the team. Such complications can influence individual military families and their reunions. But with the integration of the genders in today's military services, the unique emotional climate of each gender must be accepted and cannot be ignored.

The hero most lacking in acclaim in this scenario is the husband of the female service member. His face most often appears in the family portrait in which the wife and mother is a member of the National Guard subject to call-up, although he also may be the spouse of a wife on active duty or a Reservist who has been recalled to serve and to deploy. Regularly employed or not, advocate of the non-traditional marriage or not, he has his hands full keeping home and family functioning during her absence and frequently having to learn new tasks to do so. The male spouse might expect his wife to resume previous roles as wife and mother right after her return from a deployment or from combat that may have radically changed her. Resulting tension in the family may require professional intervention.

Meeting of the Minds

Post-deployment reunion is the time for negotiations to take place. This is different from *compromise*. Compromise occurs when each party gives in or gives up something in order to tolerate the other party. The result is a conclusion that is less than either wants—for the sake of getting along. *Negotiation* is a process that permits each party to express hopes and dreams while the other actively listens. Then the process is reciprocated as often as needed. The end result is often much better than either party expected, because, in the exchange, the reasons for each position have been explored, and each has had the opportunity to learn from the other. This is indeed "an exchange of gifts," in which gifts are the insights as well as the needs of each partner. After a prolonged separation with imperfect means of communication, each spouse has many things to teach and to learn from the other. When children are involved and their welfare, routine, and discipline are being considered, negotiation needs to be used between parents. Once parents have had their discussions, negotiation can be used between them and each child as part of the reunion process. It softens the parental role without compromising it, because all parties are honored. Negotiation requires patience and active listening skills (as explored in Part Two, Section A: VIII. A. 2 - *Negotiation*, and VI. - *Active Listening*).

With the return of the service member after a prolonged absence and subsequent changes in the structure of family living, the long-awaited returnee could easily take on the guise of "the bad guy." (For example, "When your father/mother gets home, things are going to be different around here!") Even in the routine of family living, when children (or relatives) are not satisfied with the responses to a request from one parent, they may ask the other parent, hoping for greater leniency. There needs to be an expectation that parents will consult one another and come up with a common solution to controversies when at all possible, so that the parental bond may be reestablished afresh in the minds of all concerned.

I have called the process of seeking out the easiest parent *Wedging*. This can be expected to occur when an adult member reenters the family, and the balance that was disturbed when he/she left is again subject to change. Youngsters (and some relatives) seeking their own way, challenge the unity of the authority of family leadership. Every change seems to invite testing, and youngsters will struggle to determine for themselves the strength and unity of the family structure. Driving a *wedge* is a means of testing the strength of the bond between reuniting parents. This is rarely motivated by ill intent, but rather in search of the boundaries of the family—which children need to know, because the family is their world. It would be frightening for the healthy child if the family were found to be weak or fragmented. Once any doubts have been resolved, probing is quickly minimized.

Family leadership involves the management of finances. As easier communication resumes with the return of the service member, there needs to be an amicable settlement regarding by whom and how money will be spent, saved, and recorded. One of the couple may be more talented in accounting, while the other needs to be involved in major decisions and have the ability to function financially without feeling subservient. There is no absolute right or wrong way to administer family finances, but without adjusting a plan in this area, control of the funds (and of the marriage) could be a matter of contest rather than one of mutual trust.

Mental Health Issues

Although it is rare that a mental health issue may emerge as evident in either party in the reunion of a military couple, it needs to be explored here. Many deployments overseas or at sea are quite routine, and overreactions are not appropriate. But if a radical change in behavior or in thinking is observed by those closest to the returnee or observed by the returnee in those whom he/she finds at home, attempts need to be made to share such observations at first with the person of concern. If such communications yield no positive result, help should be sought from someone in authority.

Rage has been proven to augment one's effectiveness in combat. But when the transition has been made to safety and this survival mechanism remains where it is no longer needed, guidance is required. Also, mistrust can develop in the mind of one deployed.[2] Dr. Shay writes: "Good-enough nurturance in childhood produces social trust as a matter of course; bad-enough trauma at *any* age destroys it."[3] Some experiences in addition to combat that can destroy social trust are: being held beyond one's pledged commitment to military service by "stop loss," multiple overseas tours required of National Guard soldiers recruited for domestic defense, or multiple tour extensions without explanation.

Jim Dooley, a mental health counselor with the VA in Vermont and a Viet Nam veteran, is quoted regarding problems adjusting to being back home. "What we (veterans) are saying is 'You have no idea what the other part of the world is like, and I do. And you should know it.' ...I think that's where the anger is – it's that their value systems have been fundamentally changed by that experience. And they keep that value system the rest of their life."[4]

Loyalty is sacrosanct in the military creed because of the ever-present need for protection by one's colleagues (whose entrusted duty it is "to watch your back"). Thus betrayal by a peer or a leader can be the source of greatest disillusionment. Although betrayal of either spouse by the other is known to happen, this is perceived as a *huge,* perhaps unforgivable, infraction in this population. Additionally, the linkage of past *unrelated* rage or *transferred* ghosts of mistrust can bring undeserved harm to the reuniting family, and needs to be acknowledged and dealt with promptly. If this condition persists, it needs to be diagnosed and treated promptly by abreaction therapy and/or with anger management – and with temporary enforced separation, if safety is a factor.

On the other hand, many returning soldiers who are quite conscious of violations of social trust return energized to right social wrongs. Their internalized social conscience has driven them into volunteer or employed community service, and many have sought further education and changes in career both in and outside the military. I have observed this force in the lives of many veterans, and indeed in my own experience. We might call this an acceptable and healthy response to social needs, yet despite this "acceptability," the insights and motivations of the service person and what social deficiencies have meant to him or her should not be ignored or suppressed.

Self-medication with narcotics and/or alcohol for escape from painful deployment memories and/or reactions to perceived inequities also requires prompt identification and professional attention. Treatment may or may not be indicated in every case. Conscious or unconscious *denial* by loved ones of observable post-deployment irregularities in a family member following deployment-separation is common, because one does not wish them to exist. However, love that is genuine is tough, and seeks help when others do not want to get involved.

Issues of special concern would be such things that did not exist prior to departure and that seem to dominate the returnee. Reckless behavior could reflect a continued longing for the adrenaline rush from the risks of the deployment or the experiences of combat. The following anecdote appeared in *Navy Times*.[5] Army Sergeant Joshua Chitwood, "a single 22-year-old from Ponca City, Okla., had just returned in July from 15 months in Iraq when, on a visit home to see his family, he felt an itch that needed scratching. 'I went out and bought a fast motorcycle, just to feel that rush, that high level of alertness,' said the cannoneer...." However, the opposite behavior could be manifest—withdrawal from all human relationships. "Recovery happens only in community," according to Dr. Shay.[6] If changes in behavior are significant to observers, they are signals for concern. There are also a myriad of symptoms that are incorporated under the diagnosis of PTSD: nightmares, flashbacks, rage or agitation, inappropriate avoidance of experiences that might even remotely replicate the initial trauma, or persisting depression.

The bottom line for the military family in reunion is that when issues surface in which psychological treatment appears relevant, seek professional advice. If the service member refuses to act on his/her own behalf, loved ones need to insist that competent diagnosis and treatment be sought as soon as possible. Real emotional problems do not usually get better by just waiting. Unfortunately, there needs to be honest recognition that a mental health concern may involve unfair additional risks to the service member: threats to unit comradeship, as well as to his/her advancement and career prospects. Whereas physical wounds attract sympathy, frequently emotional wounds are called "crazy," and the victims considered unreliable. However, therapeutic help must be a matter of priorities for families in reunion, and safety to self and others must be primary.

According to an episode in a series by Ted Koppel on *Nightline*, women soldiers especially have resisted mental health treatment.[7] This evidently is in response to the cultural stereotype that females are more emotional than males. Thus many women, thinking that they need to demonstrate their qualifications to serve along with the men, are prone to keep silent in the face of their own post-deployment needs.

There is always the danger that with the military, the need for psychotherapy and rehabilitation may be denied or oversimplified. The admission of the need for mental health services has always been scorned in the ranks as weakness and tantamount to loss of promotion potential and a premature end to a military career. This denial was especially emphasized by Koppel in his *Nightline* series on stress in the military.[8] An editorial in *Navy Times* dealt with the resistance of military personnel to the seeking of psychiatric care, "and combat vets most at risk were only half as likely to seek help."[9] This Editorial quotes Dr. Matthew J. Friedman in the *New England Journal of Medicine*: "They (are) apparently afraid to seek assistance for fear that a scarlet P would be attached to their careers.... If you can't cope with combat, if you don't shut up and soldier on, you will be humiliated; you and your career will be ruined." The Editorial continues: "It's not hard to see why. Consider the saga of Army Staff Sgt. Georg-Andreas Pogany: After seeing the gruesome remains of an enemy combatant while assigned to a Special Forces unit in Iraq (in October 2003), the translator was stricken with panic attacks and went to his command for help. Instead, the Army charged him with cowardice. The charges later were reduced to dereliction of duty, and his case is still in limbo." Similar cases exist.

Although I have described symptoms that can recur from either witnessing or having been exposed to trauma, the term "Post-traumatic Stress Disorder" and the civilian equivalent term "Critical Incident Stress," are used only rarely in this book. I have preferred to refer to specific symptoms by name. This is because I think that PTSD has become a popular umbrella diagnosis that seems to cover everything, to the detriment of the specific needs of individuals. There is currently a wealth of good material on the subject beyond the scope of this writing, which is readily available for the clinician and the interested reader.

Much is currently in the media concerning emotional problems of the returnees from participation in combat. The debilitating effects on veterans and their families – both physical and emotional—even made itself a theme of a daily contemporary comic strip, Garry Trudeau's opinionated *Doonesbury*.[10] This cartoon series championed the cause of returning disabled veterans during the first two weeks of January 2005 (before turning its focus to themes primarily criticizing the war). According to an Associated Press report, Army studies reveal "divorce rates as high as 21 percent among couples where one spouse has been sent off to war."[11] I believe that military marriages were at greater risk during and after Viet Nam deployments because of the impact of negative public attitudes toward the war and the effect this had on some spouses at home. Questionnaires were distributed among active duty couples and veterans of this and past wars, as research for the writing of this chapter. In their replies, some Viet Nam veterans believe their broken relationships had been influenced by a loss of confidence at home in the war they were fighting. The general confidence in support of the troops in the present conflicts will have a positive effect on the loyalty and support of families of those deployed in the Middle East. Although the current public focus is primarily on troops returning from Iraq and Afghanistan, our military stands guard in many lands and seas and in the airspace above them. Professional duties in the Armed Forces everywhere always involve stress, risk, and the unexpected. Terrorism works, because it claims no boundaries. Throughout my service as a Navy chaplain with the fleet and the Fleet Marine Force, I observed that mental health needs are not restricted to combat action.

Best Friends

Couples and families who stick together to support each other through separations required by mandated missions of the United States must be best friends. Deployment-related responsibilities can make strong friends stronger. But the best friend of all best friends when the separation is over is *time*—the gift of time. According to Holy Scripture:

For everything there is a season,
 and a time for every matter under heaven:
A time to be born, and a time to die; a time to plant,
 and a time to pluck up what is planted;
A time to kill, and a time to heal; a time to break down,
 and a time to build up;
A time to weep, and a time to laugh; a time to mourn,
 and a time to dance.[12]

When the long journey is over, there is a time to heal and a time to dance. But not so fast! First there must be time to understand, and understanding takes time. Changes have occurred through all the experiences that have happened, and all of the struggles that have been endured at home and abroad. With the advent of air transportation, reunions happen suddenly, almost intrusively. Family reunions can happen like lightning, and, although long anticipated, they can require shocking adjustments. To this can be added the impact of the sudden return of the deployed one to the homeland and to the civilian culture in which the family is immersed. When the door of the aircraft is finally opened, or when that long line of sailors pours excitedly off the gangways and the embraces occur, homecoming has just begun. *Time* is a couple's—a family's—best friend, and *Time* needs to be welcomed as well as the service member into the events of homecoming.

Picture the mobile that decorates a house. It finds beauty in the balance of its arms and weights in times of calm and even when the wind blows. But if a piece of the mobile is removed, the mobile will collapse; if a member is added, the mobile will be out of balance once again. The difference between the sticks and ornaments of a decorative mobile and a family is that the latter is a living thing. When a shift in the balance of a family is anticipated, resistance will be experienced in order to keep the family in balance. Change may be necessary; change may be for the best, but change is always scary. And change in a living, breathing family causes adjustments, if a balance is to be maintained. This is why the human family needs time to adjust to the goings and comings of one of its leaders. Each member of a family-in-balance, no matter how old or young they may be, needs to think through what is required of him or her to accommodate the departure, and then the return of the service member. This is what is called maintaining the homeostatic balance of a living entity.

One's company or platoon, one's flight crew, or one's division or ship constitutes a "second family" developed during time together and throughout deployment. Gordon Trowbridge, in an article from Camp Fallujah, Iraq, quotes Marine Pfc. Francesca Langston, of Orlando, Florida.[13] She says: "Your platoon becomes your family. All you've really got out here is who you are with." This is the same for those deployed in the military on land, sea, or air anywhere in the world. Upon return, if there are stresses at home, it is all too tempting to return to the barracks, the hangar, or the ship to find friends, thus to avoid the adjustments of homecoming. Adjustments are required of every family member to keep the family balance during times of change. Much of this may require a shift in physical accommodations, but most of this occurs in the unconscious processes of each mind involved. Some things may not be heard or seen, nor are they physically evident. But a new baby meeting its daddy for the first time may scream in honest fright. No secret here! It all takes time. Time is the best friend of best friends. Thus time needs to play its part in a parent's or an adult child's return to the fold.

An anonymous questionnaire has been mentioned that was circulated among selected service members and veterans—young and old—in the preparation of this chapter. It asked for answers to four basic questions: what were the best and the worst things that were experienced in the post-deployment reunion with the spouse; and, if there were children, with them. Few answers with depth were forthcoming from those who had recently returned to their families from deployment. A myopia or near-sightedness seems to exist when we are very close to an experience. In stark contrast, significant responses were returned on questionnaires from veterans and spouses who had experienced deployments and reunions in World War II, in the Korean and Viet Nam conflicts. These veterans and their spouses seemed to be able to reflect and easily report on what was asked. This demonstrates that understanding the post-deployment reunion experience requires time for insights to mature. The rhetorical question is asked: Does it not take time for us to understand some of the greatest experiences in our lives?

Weeks, months, even 10 years down the road will reveal the deepest meanings of such experiences as working and living apart in support of, and in the rendering of military service, then putting family life back together at the end of the long trail. I add whimsically that even Navy coffee takes time to percolate.

---

1. Kim van Meter, "In the Trenches," *Oakdale* (California) *Leader* (September 15, 2004): A-1, A-11.
2. Jonathan Shay, *Odysseus in America: Combat Trauma and the Trials of Homecoming* (New York: Scribner, 2002), xv, 4, 140, 158-60.
3. Ibid., 176.
4. Raney Aronson, "The Soldier's Heart," *Frontline* (WGBH, March 1, 2005). The text of the October 5, 2004 interview with Jim Dooley related to the television program may be found on the internet at *http://www.pbs.org/wgbh/pages/frontline/shows/heart/interviews/dooley.html*.
5. Lloyd Francis, Jr., "On the Edge: Returning Troops Crave Rush of War Zone Adrenaline," *Navy Times* (October 18, 2004): 41-42.
6. Shay, *Odysseus*, 4.
7. Ted Koppel, "Coming Home: Invisible Casualties," *Nightline* (ABC-TV, 3rd episode in a series of 3, December 17, 2004).
8. Ibid., 1st episode, December 15, 2004.

9. Editorial, "Treating Troop's Emotional Wounds," *Navy Times* (July 19, 2004): 44.

10. Garry Trudeau, *Doonesbury* (Universal Press Syndicate, January 2-15, 2005). The third of G. B. Trudeau's trilogy of somber cartoon characters depicts his combat veteran in rehabilitation: *The Long Road Home: One Step at a Time* (Kansas City: Andrews McMeel Publishing, 2005). Proceeds from this book will benefit Fisher House Foundation that provides hospitality homes adjacent to military medical facilities for relatives accompanying injured service members.

11. Kimberly Hefling, "Army Tries to Save Marriages," *Associated Press* in (Redding, California) *Record Searchlight* (December 30, 2004): A-1, A-7.

12. *Ecclesiastes* 3:1-4.

13. Gordon Trowbridge, "We Have to Make Every Day Christmas," *Navy Times* (December 27, 2004): 11.

PART TWO—PRE-REUNION SEMINARS

Section A:

Seminar for Returning Groups

Section B:

Seminar for Spouses

Note: Part Two is also available in the attached DVD for printing in 8.5" x 11" format. This is to accommodate Facilitators, who may punch the pages on the left side for 3-hole binder use, placing the materials on a lectern while leading Seminar(s).

SECTION A:

PRE-REUNION SEMINAR FOR RETURNING UNIT/
SHIPBOARD GROUPS

**Title of presentation:
"It's All in the (Service Branch) Family"**

This Seminar is provided for deployed units just prior to arriving home. It is recommended that the first group(s) be held for officers, the second group(s) for senior Non-Commissioned Officers, then for other Enlisted Personnel in the groups that follow. For Navy Battle Groups and Marines afloat, it is to be given at sea in several seminars on each returning ship, beginning with the Officers' Ward Room, then Chiefs' Mess, and then several for married and engaged Enlisted Personnel in groups. This sequence provides the benefit of the seminar first to seniors/supervisors, as well as providing them access to the material prior to it being conducted for those whom they supervise. The size of the groups may well be determined by the space available, and by the needs of the attendees as determined by their leaders. A complementary Seminar (see Section B) is planned for spouses awaiting the return of their service member. It is to be held somewhat in advance of the Seminar for the troops, so that a portion of their responses planned as part of the presentation for the returnee's may reach their Seminar Facilitators (by message, preferably) prior to the conduct of the Seminar for those returning from deployment.

Seminar Contact Time: 2.5 Hours

Properties Check List and Packing List for Presenter(s) in remote locations:

___ Scripts ___ Mobile Model ___ "Jimmy Script" (see XI. Sect. A)
___ Wives' Responses (sent from Home Base/Homeport)
___ Footprint (see XI.B.4) ___ Bell Timer ___ Water Glass
___ 2 Films/Videos (on attached DVD) ___ Masking Tape
___ 2 Tripods (for Newsprint Pads) ___ 2 Rolls of Newsprint
___ Felt-tip Markers: ___Blue ___Red ___Black ___Purple ___Green

___ *-Equipment for projecting films (such as DVD, VHS, or 16mm)
___ *-Laptop for DVD (or Take-up Reel for 16mm)
___ *-Extension Cord
___ *-Projection Screen (or use bed sheet)

*-Coffee Mess:
___ Card or Mess Table
___ Trash Can(s) with plastic bag inserts
___ 2 or 3 Pots (Coffee & Hot Water)
___ Stir Sticks ___ Coffee ___Tea ___ Chocolate
___ Cream ___ Sugar ___Cups

___ Film #1: "Ordinary People" (last 18 minutes of film only) Available on attached DVD, or at the University of Pittsburgh, Center for Instructional Resources: Call Number F-927.

___ Film #2: "Nurturing" Available on attached DVD, or from Davidson Films, 735 Tank Farm Road, Suite 210, San Luis Obispo, CA 93401.

[*-items to pre-arrange for use at site]

ABOUT THE FILMS TO BE USED IN THE SEMINARS

Ordinary People: A Film about Child Abuse (1978) is available through the University of Pittsburgh, Center for Instructional Resources, under Call Number F-927. The Parental Stress Center, 5877 Commerce Street, Pittsburgh, PA 15206 (www.PSCFamily.net) co-produced and holds the copyright for this film, and has granted permission for its duplication and use with Part Two of this book. This film was originally created in 16mm format, but a DVD format is attached for the convenience of projecting it in remote locations. The intent of the screenwriters was for the training of Social Workers and Visiting Nurses in the identification of impending child abuse, thus for purposes of the Pre-Reunion Seminars, it is recommended that <u>only the final two-thirds (approximately 23 minutes) of the film be used</u>, as in the attached DVD. (It is best to start at the scene under the bridge where the engineers are conferring about "twinning" the structure. A barge is towed in the background on the river.) Our objective is to demonstrate the importance of the active listening skills taught in the seminar—<u>not</u> to suggest that child abuse is suspected. At the conclusion of the showing, if in a darkened space, a few minutes of delay is suggested before the lights are turned up. This is to avoid embarrassment of those who might be moved by the presentation, and to allow the urgent lesson it conveys to "sink in." Past experience with these Seminars indicates that <u>this film is NOT RECOMMENDED for use with the Spouses' Seminar (Part Two, Section B)</u>.

Nurturing (1978) was produced by and is available from Davidson Films, Inc., 735 Tank Farm Road, Suite 210, San Luis Obispo, CA 93401 (www.davidsonfilms.com). Their telephone is (805) 594-0422; FAX (805) 594-0532. This program is available in VHS, is 17 minutes in length, but it has been attached in DVD format for convenience of projecting. This is absolutely the best the Author has ever reviewed on child care! The program is fast-moving with delightful sound, and the Part Two, Section A text of the Pre-Reunion Seminar presents a systematic means of involving the audience in a review of each teaching vignette. Although the subjects are of pre-school age, the Section A text of the Seminar provides an optional section by which the film can be applied to the care of older children including teenagers. This video is essential for both the Seminar for the returning troops (Section A), and the Seminar for the waiting spouses (Section B).

IT'S ALL IN THE (Army, Navy, Marine Corps, Air Force, Coast Guard) FAMILY

I. Introduction

    A. Commanding Officer (or Executive Officer) welcomes, introduces Seminar, or Facilitator #1 introduces Facilitator #2, who introduces Facilitator #3, who explains and introduces the Seminar.

    B. Time discipline necessary for best results (Explained by Facilitator #1):

        1. Do not scatter at the 2 breaks, Begin together, Coffee & Latrine are near

        2. Rapid Response is requested to Questions and Exercises—"Get involved"

II. Didactic (Initial teaching)

    A. Family Dynamics

        1. "When you say 'My Family,' who are you talking about?" [Facilitator urges rapid responses] Service Member rarely includes *Self*!

        2. A "mobile" (*art construction*) is both described and displayed, and is used to describe family upon departure and re-entry; tends to *unbalance the mobile*. If this were a <u>living model</u> it would resist change to stay balanced.

a.) At departure: Resistance of family
(Appeals expressed or imagined)

b.) On Return: They have to set another place at the table; finding your tools; what jobs for the family (both needed and usurped by others) can you resume?

c.) There is that "Second Mobile," the friends in the company or the ship that is a 2nd Family, which can be a ready retreat from home/family

3. Internal dialogue described:

a.) When others at home have grown (and assumed new responsibilities) "Am I needed?"

b.) Response to Wives' Meeting displayed; they say: "Yes, you are!"

c.) But we still may ask: "Am I needed?"

B. Stability for each Service Member of the unit or ship as "2nd Family" or "2nd Mobile"

1. Shared Experiences and Common Language

2. "I am needed at the unit or on the ship."

a.) Comrades: work together, have fun together, "shoot the bull" together b.) Demands of work continue (Go UA or miss movement, find out you are really needed.)

      c.) Temptation (imagined or expressed) when decisions have to be made at home, or when sticky situations have to be resolved with family – *to retreat to the unit/ship and service comrades/shipmates rather than face matters in the family.* "They have been solving things while I was gone." Problems escalate.

III. Fantasy/Reality Trip

    A. Facilitator: "Let me take you on a Scottish vacation." (Costs nothing) One Facilitator records on Newsprint in a 2nd column with <u>Green Marker</u>, while other Facilitator takes (perhaps edits) verbal responses to: "<u>Describe life at home in your absence – use your imagination.</u>" Toward the end of the list ask for "Especially positive responses."

    B. Facilitator: "Now describe your life in the Battalion/on the Ship during this Deployment." Use same recording procedure as in "A" but in first column on newsprint using <u>Red</u> felt marker.

    C. Display Wives' List from their seminar at home, and compare lists: (Facilitator points out: Shows pride in Service Member; urges appreciation of spouse's hardships, responsibilities, loneliness and coping abilities.)

D. Didactic

    1. Coping stories about the "home front", asking "What is good about this?" Example: "You find new tires on the car that are not 'your brand.'" (Spouse kept it running in your absence, got the baby to check-ups, got the groceries, children to school, soccer, Little League, paid the bills.) Spouse's growth/initiative and children's growth will not be a threat to their needing the Service Member when he/she returns, if <u>appreciation</u> can be expressed.

    2. "Glass half full" story: (Use prop – Water Glass half full)

        a.) We live in a critical/analytical atmosphere: inspections, evaluations & Fitness Reports, making it hard to see the positives.

        b.) [Navy example] On return home, imagine the 1.MC announcing: "Ogre arriving, knock off all card games, silence about the decks, Liberty is secured until after inspection" vs. Appreciation.

    3. It can be deduced from the <u>Fantasy Trip Lists</u> that we cannot perfectly know or feel what it has been like for the spouse/family during deployment/separation period. Therefore, a *Debriefing* with letters and a "Listening-Telling" opportunity early in the homecoming reunion is necessary – so Spouse/Family Members and Service Member can be understood and appreciated.

4. "The Honeymoon"

   a.) If sex is to be the initial priority, mutual agreement will bring maximum pleasure and fulfillment. Examples: <u>A Service Member</u>: "The second thing I am going to do when I get home is take my hat off!" <u>A Service Wife</u>: "When my husband returns, I will not be ready to go to bed with a stranger."

   b.) Sharing of experiences and hopes, and the making of plans for the future will be the foundation upon which the future of the marriage and family depends. Uniting the lives of a couple in reunion consists of... *Emotions:* What each has experienced during the separation, and feelings connected with each experience. *Intellect:* What each has learned during the separation. *Spirituality:* Where each has progressed in regard to their Faith Group. *Sexuality:* Will be most meaningful when the couple are at one with the other elements of their common life.

SECTION A *Seminar for Returning Groups* 69

IV. Situational Prototypes (An exercise)

  A. Form <u>Groups of 5</u>, each with a <u>Spokesperson</u>

  B. Introduce <u>3 questions</u>, using newsprint, and ensuring <u>Groups</u> understand how to apply them to Situations that will follow:
    1. "What is GOOD about it?
    2. "What are the POTENTIAL PROBLEMS?"
    3. "What SOLUTIONS would you suggest?"

  C. Explain: <u>Plenary Feedback</u> (reporting) will be requested after each Situation has been discussed by Groups.

  D. Explain: <u>Situations</u> take place in an imaginary family while Service Member is deployed.

  E. Introduce the Situations one at a time, each one after previous Situation has been discussed by Groups, but not necessarily reported by Spokesperson. Reporting on each can come from Groups after all have been introduced.

    1. <u>Situation #1:</u> "Mother has kids kiss Service Member's life-size picture every night at bedtime." (For Couples with no children: "Spouse kisses your life-size picture.")

      a.) Introduce Situation #1 for Groups to discuss.

b.) For Facilitators only: Anticipated responses from Groups:
(+) Keeps absent parent "alive," preserves expression of affection.
(-) Idolization leads to fallen image on return, e.g., parent spanks, gets angry, is a real (human), etc.; changes in appearance during time away, e.g., weight change, bearded/shaved face, etc.
(Suggestions) Exchange updated photos in various activities, audio/video tapes. On return, "come in easy"–without sudden changes, <u>listen and observe</u>.

2. <u>Situation #2:</u> "When I get home, I just want to sit in front of the fire with my family and watch TV."

a.) Introduce Situation #2 for Groups to discuss.

b.) For Facilitators only: Anticipated responses from Groups:
(+) Join in the family routine (<u>if it is their routine</u>), being part of family life, "togetherness."
(-) Service Parent has been away, now wants to stay home, Spouse has been working or shut in with children, now wants to go out; TV takes the place of interpersonal communications.
(Suggestions) Find out what their routine has been; Ask what they like/want to do; Talk over what you want to do (also important to include self); <u>Negotiate</u> (cf. Below).

3. <u>Situation #3:</u> "I can't wait 'till I get home, so I can get the checkbook back and buy my new motorcycle." (Use "camper" for E-7-9; "boat" for Officer Groups.)

   a.) Introduce Situation #3 for Groups to discuss

   b.) For <u>Facilitators only</u> - Anticipated responses from Groups:
   (+) Returnee has a goal; few positives will be offered here.
   (-) Spouse's responsibilities for handling finances, perhaps a new position, not recognized and appreciated. Is a reward for deployment necessary? — Service Member is not the only one who has been deprived.
   (Suggestions) Talk it over at the right time, <u>Negotiate</u>.

V. <u>Break</u> with Coffee Mess and Latrines/Heads nearby. Give specific time for return. "We will not start until we are all together. Please be prompt."

VI. Active Listening

    A. Demonstration by 2 Facilitators. One Facilitator (Teller) asks the attention of the other Facilitator, and later in the conversation the Teller must make a decision from among several options. The subject is prearranged according to what may be relevant to the group of participants.

        1. Bad Example (acting may exaggerate the behavior for teaching purposes and because of time constraints.) "Teller" asks for the attention of the Listener and indicates an important personal concern. "Listener" slouches in chair, avoids eye contact, changes subject to matters of the Listener's interest, offers irrelevant responses.

            a.) At cut-off of dialogue, "Listener" assesses frustration of observers.

            b.) "Listener" assesses the anger of observers toward him/her (as a means of getting Facilitator out of the role—as in psychodrama.)

            c.) Facilitator asks/tells group: "Nothing like this ever happens in the military, does it." (This is commonly received with laughter.)

2. Good Example

   a.) "Teller" asks for the attention of the "Listener" as before, indicating an important personal concern. "Listener" sits erect, leaning slightly forward, establishes eye contact, demonstrates good body language.

   b.) "Teller" explores the subject of concern, "Listener" uses good Active Listening techniques, as explained in Section 3 below.

   c.) "Teller" faces a decision between options (as prearranged script); "Listener" defines the options: "On the one hand (this), and on the other hand (that)." Defines options, does not make decision. Reflects assurance in the solution of the "Teller."

3. "Listener" (now acting as Facilitator) <u>polls the group of observers</u> in an attempt to get the following responses in the order given:

   a.) BODY LANGUAGE: "Listener" sits forward, is animated, maintains eye contact, etc.

b.) "Listener" picks up first on the "Teller's" FEELINGS (explaining that the major communications link between two humans lies in the mutual acceptance of the feelings of each: e.g., comm wire between two telephones.) Example: Supervisor to angry worker: "I can see that you are up-tight. Please tell me about it." This defuses a potential explosion.

c.) REPEAT BACK at intervals by "Listener" keeps "Teller" on track.

d.) REPHRASE the material given by "Teller."

e.) Use of phrase: "DID I UNDERSTAND YOU TO SAY:...?" This assures that both "Listener" and "Teller" make corrections if there are possible misunderstandings of the content.

f.) Use of the phrase by "Listener": "I HEAR YOU." This encourages the "Teller" to advance.

g.) DEFINE THE DECISION at the point where one has to be made: "On the one hand (this); and on the other hand (that)...."

h.) In response to the inevitable question, "What should I do?" "Listener" asks: "WELL, WHAT IS YOUR PLAN?" or "WHAT DO YOU THINK YOU SHOULD DO?" This encourages the "Teller" to take responsibility.

i.) When a decision is made by the "Teller," reassure by saying: "YOU SEEM SATISFIED WITH YOUR DECISION."

B. Didactic: Newsprint (preprinted, or on Power Point slides) is now displayed with the above ITEMS IN CAPITAL LETTERS listed and explained in order. This then continues with an expanded explanation of the last 2 items, that Active Listening...

j.) IS NOT ADVICE-GIVING

(1) Facilitator: "What is wrong with 'If I were you, I would....'" Answer: "I am not you!" It is a lie; invasion of another's life.

(2) If wrong decision, shifts the blame. If right, lowers self-esteem.

k.) IS NOT PASSIVE LISTENING

(1) Without feedback, one does not know what the "silent partner" is thinking, and needs to know *where what one is telling is going and how it may be used*.

(2) Facilitator reenacts paranoia-producing role play: "Let me tell you about my Supervisor (SGT, Division Officer)" and continues with negatives. Finally, Listener reveals this is his cousin (or similar outcome).

C. Active Listening Practice (exercise)

1. With Active Listening techniques reviewed, exercise is to apply to family on homecoming.

2. Form entire group into dyads (groups of two, facing each other)

3. Set contract:

    a.) First Listener is identified (hold up hand)

    b.) Listener and Teller will switch on signal, <u>not before</u>

    c.) Time for exercise established (suggest 7.5 minutes before switch); Use audible bell-timer

    d.) Urge participants to use Active Listening skills

    e.) Display skills listed on newsprint or Power Point where all see

4. Assign subject for discussion: "What activities do I plan with my family on return."

5. Switch Teller/Listener halfway through total time; Close drill

D. Plenary Feedback from dyads (quickly):

   1. When as Teller, did you feel heard?

   2. Was it easier to talk?

   3. Did you feel good about it?

   4. What lessons were learned (or remembered)?

   5. Facilitator comments:

      a.) noise level up indicated increased participation

      b.) hearing & telling is "gift" giving and receiving, satisfies both

VII. FILM #1: "Ordinary People" using last 14 minutes of this film only, as pre-set

   A. Introductory remarks by Facilitator:

      1. This family has <u>everything</u>... except

         a.) they can't <u>listen</u> so they can understand each other

         b.) they can't <u>talk</u> so they can be heard

         c.) they talk <u>at</u> each other, not <u>to</u> each other

2. They do not pick up on <u>feelings</u>, nor do they share <u>hopes or dreams</u>. (Only the Visiting Nurse does, which shows contrast)

3. Husband is not in the military, but he surely could be!

4. This film is shown to emphasize that the Active Listening drill is not just a "touchy-feely" game, but the real stuff of life, essential to each of us and our family's happiness.

B. Show the film. (Starting scene: Engineers view bridge with river and barge in background.)

C. At the end of the film, as the credits begin, Projectionist turns sound down gradually, then turns off the projector lamp. The overhead lights are kept off for over 60 seconds.

D. Immediately after the lights go on, Facilitator #1 and Writer/Recorder (Facilitator #2) at the newsprint tripod start the next section.

VIII. Didactic on communications. Writer/Recorder transcribes underlined words below on newsprint (or projects them in order on Power Point) as they are discussed by Facilitator #1

A. "The ingredients of good communications are…"

    1. Need to <u>know what you want</u>. If one feels secure in his/her position, then it is okay with you for others to express their wants also — even if they are different from your wants or ideas.

    2. Fine art of <u>Negotiation</u> is the sharing of hopes and dreams.

        a.) Facilitator explains: Negotiation is not the same as *Compromise*. Compromise requires each party to give up some things so that they can tolerate each other. The solution is less than each would have wanted. *Negotiation* requires each to listen attentively to the other, and possibly learn from the other. They agree on what is best for both for a final answer.

        b.) Example: Spouse when Service Member returns: "Now that you are home I want to go to Europe for the summer."

        S.M.: "I just want to enjoy home and the kids and go nowhere."
        Spouse: "I have been kept at home all this time, and I need to go."

S.M.: "Okay, let's take in a movie tonight."
Spouse: "No! You don't understand. I need to get away."
S.M.: "We can't afford Europe. How about Lake Tahoe?"
Spouse: "If we can stay a week without the kids, it's okay."
S.M. "I'll get Mom to baby-sit. Okay! Let's pack."

3. <u>Teller/Listener roles</u> observed in turn (as in Active Listening)

4. Make <u>appointments</u> with those you love

   a.) To talk, to discuss, to make plans, to have a fight, to make love after the kids are asleep, to go grocery shopping together, etc.

   b.) Appointments require not only a <u>time</u>, but an appropriate <u>place</u>.

   c.) Sounds stilted perhaps, but when you have to wait on someone a lot, what message do you get about yourself? (I'm not important. Frequent example: in physician's waiting room.)

SECTION A *Seminar for Returning Groups*   81

    d.) Is it *Non-Urgent*? The very moment one gets home from work (or cruise) the whole family including the dog approaches with matters to be solved, all barking for attention! Can it wait? ...'till he/she gets the hat off? ...'till after the 5 P.M. news? ...'till after dinner?

    e.) If it cannot wait, it is *Urgent*. Example: "Our daughter is eloping!" "There is a grease fire on the stove!"

    f.) If matters wait too long, it is *Gunny-sacking:* Unsolved matters accumulate without solutions; the bag gets so full that it will explode. Example: refer to the film. [Facilitator crosses out (with an "X") the term "Gunny-sacking" on newsprint or Power Point]

5. <u>Dumping</u>, or how to solve: "I don't want to bring the job home."

    a.) Example given of how a hard day is denied at home, but how this contaminates home activities that follow: dinner, kids, etc.

    b.) Partner feels cut off, excluded from spouse's life.

    c.) Ask: "How do you cure a boil?" Expected answer: "Lance it." A moment to *debrief* to explain something of what went on to drain "the poison." (This is like taking a good dump.)

6. <u>Avoid leaks</u>. When things build up at home, it may seem easier to talk to people who are not in a position to reduce the pressure.

   a.) Ask: "Who hears more confessions than priests do?"

   Anticipated answer: "bartenders, barbers and hairdressers, fellow soldiers/shipmates, mothers, bridge/mah-jong friends"

   b.) ...rather than spouses (refer to "The Second Mobile")

   c.) Lets off pressure temporarily, but solves nothing. (Often heard: "I feel so much better after talking to you." But... should you, if nothing has changed?)

7. <u>Terminology</u> can invite or avoid conflict. Using a trout fishing story, illustrate that *Words* can be used as bait when fishing for a fight:

   a.) Wrong Way! Exercise: "Imagine it is the end of a long day or deployment. *Without thinking*, what is your *first thought* when asked:

      (1) "How would like to go to the commissary?" (Not at all! Should I lie to please?)

      (2) "Why don't <u>you</u> do the dishes?" (I don't know – I'm a dummy; Guilty again)

SECTION A *Seminar for Returning Groups*   83

(3) "You <u>must</u> wash the car!"...<u>ought to</u> ... <u>should</u> wash (Who says so?!)

(4) "Wives cook, all the other husbands mow the lawn." (Who cares. I'm not "just another husband.")

(5) "If you love me, you'll take me out tonight." (It's cheaper in Naples. ...or in Okinawa.)

(6) "Remember what I told you about your dirty laundry?" (No! I'm dumb, so tell me if you're so smart.)

(7) "My father (or mother) always fixed breakfast for me." (So, ...let 'em! I guess I don't measure up.)

Every one of these requests holds a <u>Hidden Message</u> about the Listener. Although it may be *unconscious,* it is bait for a fight.

b.) Right Way! Not "How would you like to do the dishes?"
But instead, use...*THREE MAGIC WORDS* - to which the Listener may not react (hearing "obey"), but is more inclined to listen <u>because Negotiation can follow</u>:
Request: "I WOULD LIKE...you to do the dishes."
Answer: "I AM (AM NOT) WILLING..."
Other options:

"<u>I am willing</u> to wash. <u>I would like</u> you to dry them."

"<u>I am willing</u> to do them in the morning when I am rested."

"<u>I am willing</u> to go down the hall with you and remind the kids that it is their night to do them."

(1) "I" message, not "You" Message. No unconscious need for the Listener to defend self

(2) Not an order or a demand

(3) Listener does not feel obligated because of his/her status

(4) It can be NEGOTIATED!

<u>Summary:</u> "Magic Wand Negotiating" is the art of sharing hopes and building dreams together.

IX. Handling Anger

    A. Stand the Group, Stretch: Feel the surge of Energy. Then be seated. "ANGER IS ENERGY" (Facilitator writes this title on newsprint)

B. Didactic:

   1. Energy is potentially *good*.

      a.) Anger is energy; therefore anger is potentially good

      b.) Like any energy source, it needs to be <u>harnessed and directed</u>

   2. Humans have been given Anger-Energy for the purpose of solving problems

      a.) Cats use Anger-Energy for "fight or flight." Cats are smart

      b.) All too often, Humans use Anger-Energy against themselves
      Example: One feels a shaking sensation when Angry = potential energy; Many angry persons will hit a locker or wall, drink too much, strike out at authority unadvisedly

      c.) St. Paul advised: "Be angry, but sin not." (Ephesians 4:26)

C. Continue to draw on newsprint below "Anger is Energy" an illustration relevant to the understanding of the participants, such as a pressure cooker, over inflation of a pneumatic tire, or a marine boiler

1. Naval Boiler example (Figure 1):

    a.) <u>Draw (as first step only)</u>: Closed drum; Water half full; Bunsen burner with fuel source (gas hose); flame under closed drum. Facilitator asks: <u>What will happen?</u> Explosion, Blow up! <u>Have you ever been so angry that you have "blown up?</u>" "I know this never happens in the military (or on the USS Neversail)!"

    b.) <u>Draw</u> (hastily): Up-takes, throttle valve, turbine, gears, shaft, propeller, etc. showing a system designed to do a job for which it was intended, e.g., move the ship.

    c.) Facilitator asks: "If 600 p.s.i. were expanded in a 450-pound system, or 1200 p.s.i. in a 600-pound system...<u>What would happen</u>? Gaskets & Gland Seals blow, erode turbine blades, and if governor is not tripped, *this will damage the system.* <u>Have you ever tried to solve a problem</u> when you have been so steamed up that you have blown the very resources that were designed to help you? ...angered the very people that could have helped you? ...and blown it?

SECTION A *Seminar for Returning Groups* 87

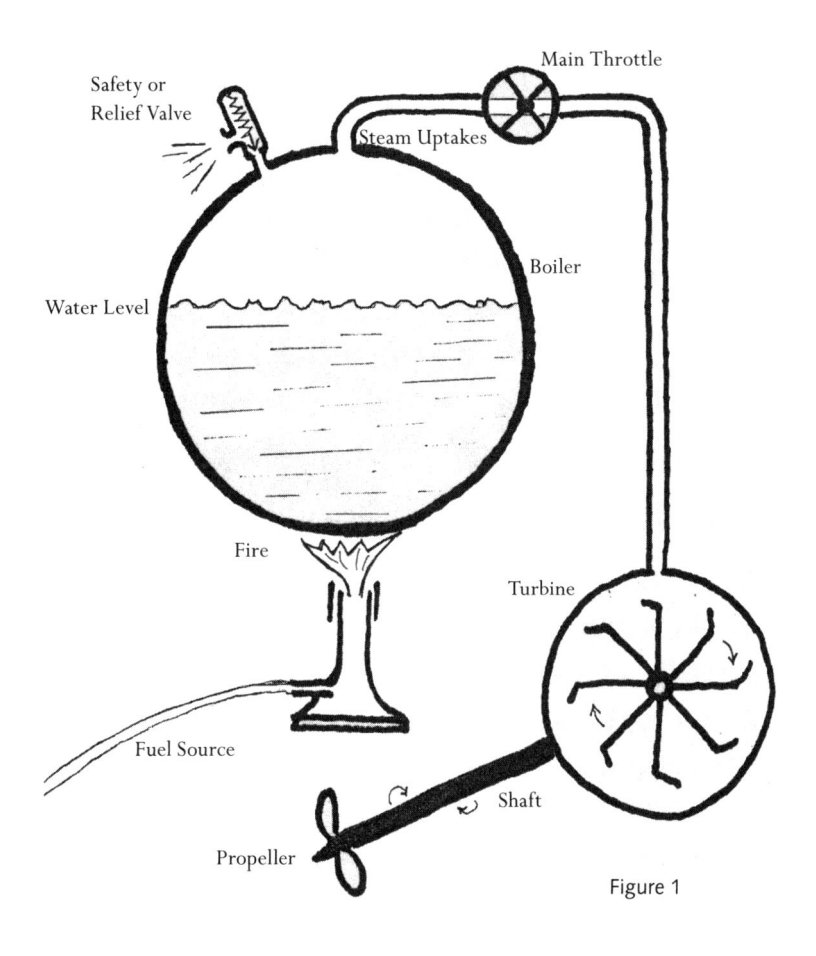

Figure 1

- Safety or Relief Valve
- Main Throttle
- Steam Uptakes
- Boiler
- Water Level
- Fire
- Fuel Source
- Turbine
- Shaft
- Propeller

d.). <u>Question:</u> "What does our system need to prevent this?" <u>Answer:</u> "A relief or safety valve." [Now add safety valve to newsprint]

2. When one has an excess of Anger-Energy, how can one blow off steam, that is, get rid of excess PHYSICAL ENERGY?

   a.) Frequent advice: "Sit down and cool off; you'll get over it." NO! This could take forever. Maybe one shouldn't get over it with nothing solved. But trying to solve with too much energy will not help.

   b.) Physical exercise brings pressure down to where it can be controlled. Run, pump iron, do push-ups, etc.

   c.) Exercise doesn't solve the problem, but it <u>doesn't do damage either</u>.

3. <u>Question</u>: "If the relief valve sticks open, what will happen?" <u>Answer</u>: "All the energy will escape, and nothing will be left to do the job, solve a conflict (or power the ship). However, when the excess pressure is relieved, it is time to open the throttle.

D. Story: "The Drill Instructor and his kids"

   1. Inspector of Recruits: All day long: "Clean up your mess!" "Gear drift!"

   2. Same thing at home. This was more than he could take.

3. I met him when he was under arrest and taken away from his family

4. I discussed "The Boiler" with him

5. He returned to the same job, and same home, but played it differently

6. He saw the same messes returning home. Went to back yard and did push-ups. Dad's "Yelling Tree" was forcefully called many colorful expletives

7. Although he never thought he would be doing this, he found himself on his knees with his children helping them pick up their toys.

8. Third night when he got home, children were already picking up. Why?

   a.) His children were learning their father was not "an animal."

   b.) They recognized that picking up their room was important to him.

   c.) He expended work-related anger before emotionally entering family.

X. <u>Break</u> with same instructions as before

    A. Facilitator #1 finds and instructs volunteer to be "Jimmy."

    B. Facilitator #2 prepares for the projection of Film #2

XI. "Wedging"

    A. Role play. Begin by introducing the "Cast" to the Group of observers: Facilitator #2 is Dad; Facilitator #1 is Mom (curtseys); Volunteer is Jimmy. (Applause)

    Players are given copies of the Script (as below):

    1. "Take One"

        a.) <u>Jimmy</u>: "Can I go bowling with Billy, and have him stay over tonight?"
<u>Dad</u>: "No. We'd have to drive you, and your mother and I have plans for the evening."

        b.) <u>Jimmy</u> (now in the kitchen): "Mommy?" (She greets Jimmy.) "Can I go bowling with Billy, and have him stay over tonight?"
<u>Mom</u>: "That's right, it's Thursday (a family routine when Dad is away.) Well, I suppose so. I don't think your father will mind."

c.) <u>Dad</u>: Invites Mom. "It's almost time to go, Dear."
<u>Mom</u> refuses because of Jimmy's plans.
<u>They argue</u> in front of Jimmy.

d.) <u>Dad</u>: "Never mind! I'm going to Dale's (use familiar bar's name) with the guys!!!"

e.) <u>Mom</u>: "Go! That's just the way you were before deployment."

2. "Take Two"

a.) <u>Jimmy</u>: "Can I go bowling with Billy, and have him stay over tonight?" "I need to know NOW!"

b.) Dad delays a decision. "Your mother and I will talk it over." Jimmy is asked to wait in the living room while…

c.) <u>Mom and Dad</u> *NEGOTIATE* in private. Then together they listen to Jimmy and *NEGOTIATE* with him.

d.) <u>Suggested closing dialogue:</u> "Math tests have been bad. We think we need to change the family routine. Please study tonight. Friday after school you can go bowling with Billy, have pizza and spend the night and watch TV. Tonight, homework. Mom and Dad are stepping out."

e.) <u>Jimmy</u> gets a better "deal" and consents.

f.) <u>Observers</u> are prompted to applaud the actors.

B. Didactic: "Wedging Explained"

1. Display and explain drawing on newsprint: Cross-section of log or rock being split by a V-shaped Wedge (Figure 2)

2. Facilitator: "In the Role Play we see the testing of limits — which if not checked could drive a wedge between parents"

     a.) It is natural for children to probe the limits which define their world, especially <u>when a parent returns from a long absence,</u> or when any other changes take place in the family structure. Limits can mean care and concern.

     b.) When a newborn infant is picked up by one supporting its back and head only, it will throw its arms back to determine its *Support System*

     c.) When a Parent returns from a deployment, each Child's Support System is perceived to undergo a change. <u>Testing of boundaries occurs</u>

          (1) ...to define limits (and to probe for changes)

          (2) ...to reassure the existence of a "new Support System." So, this is normal and to be <u>expected</u>.

SECTION A *Seminar for Returning Groups* 93

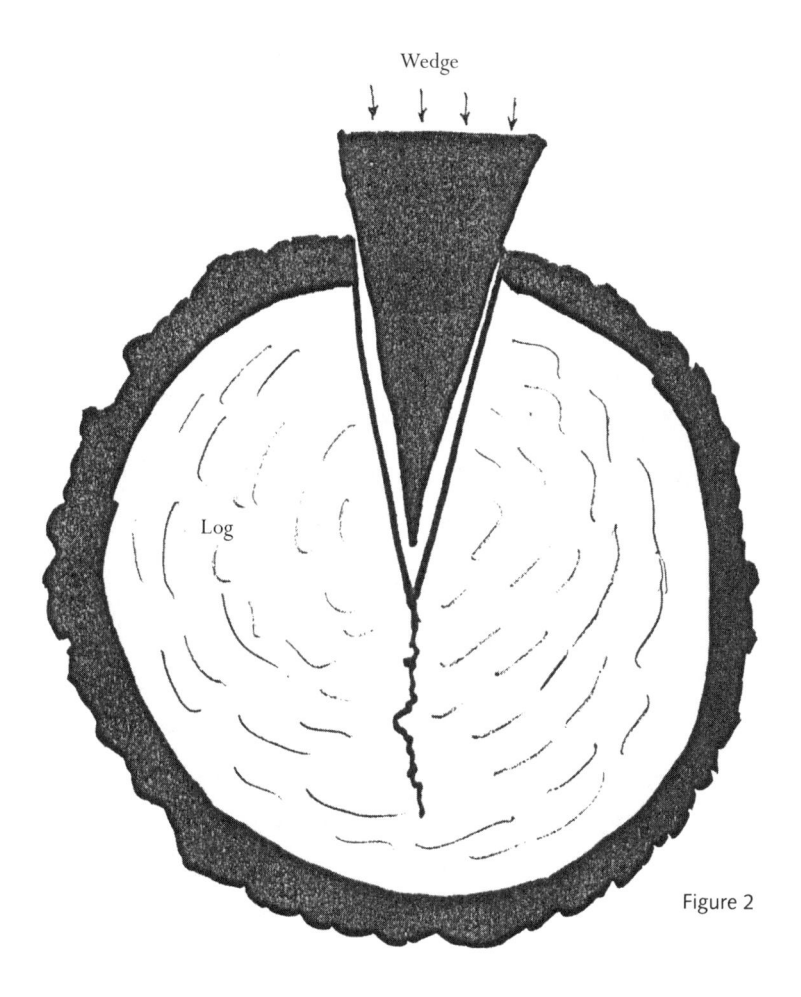

Wedge

Log

Figure 2

3. Two stereotypes describe possible causes of parental disagreement on "child management" when a parent returns from deployment:

   a.) Spouse with children at home becomes tired of controlling, wears down, and things become too relaxed, or sets a routine that works when

one parent is in charge. Returnee has lived
in a very disciplined and structured military
life, and may face differences at home

b.) Parent at home has maintained structure in
the absence of the Service Member, and needs
appreciation for doing this. Service Member
has been missing the children, wants their
affection, and tends to be too easy with them,
compromising family routine of discipline

<u>Summary:</u> Both need each other's
help and advice to provide a balance of
the support structure with gentleness
and rapport with children

c.) <u>Inconsistency in parenting</u> is the matrix
of delinquency and mental illness

4. MYTH: "Chivalry" demands that the man make
the decisions, carry all burdens, which is culturally
outmoded in our modern world of equality. Should
one declare (male or female): "I mean to be the <u>Head
of my household,</u>" what is being demanded? Posturing
Exercises:

a.) *Piggyback Carriage.* Results: locus of pain;
heavy load; spouse never learns to walk;
both learn to resent this, which causes
"nonsense fights," and/or sudden separation

b.) *King of the Mountain.* The would-be dominant person stands on chair with one foot on the back of the one acting as the spouse. [Use footprint paper so as not to dirty clothing of actor (Figure 3).] Results: Initial ego trip, but shaky position which relies on the spouse for stability (who can knock "dominant one" off the pedestal in a heartbeat); spouse's growth threatens relationship, so spouse must either grow or collapse under the weight

c.) *Object of Worship.* (Dominant spouse still stands on chair, submissive spouse assumes posture of prayer to the other.) Results: Initial ego trip, but a lonely position because no one dares touch a god

d.) Two Military Models (explained, but not postured):

  (1) CO (Service Member), XO (Spouse), Troops (Children)

  (2) Staff Model: Advisors to the General/Admiral

e.) "The position you would like with your Spouse" Allow volunteers to choose by posturing. Usually: Two standing tall together, who spontaneously touch each other's lives when they wish to do so. Virginia Satir: "It is not the tie that binds, but the bond that connects."

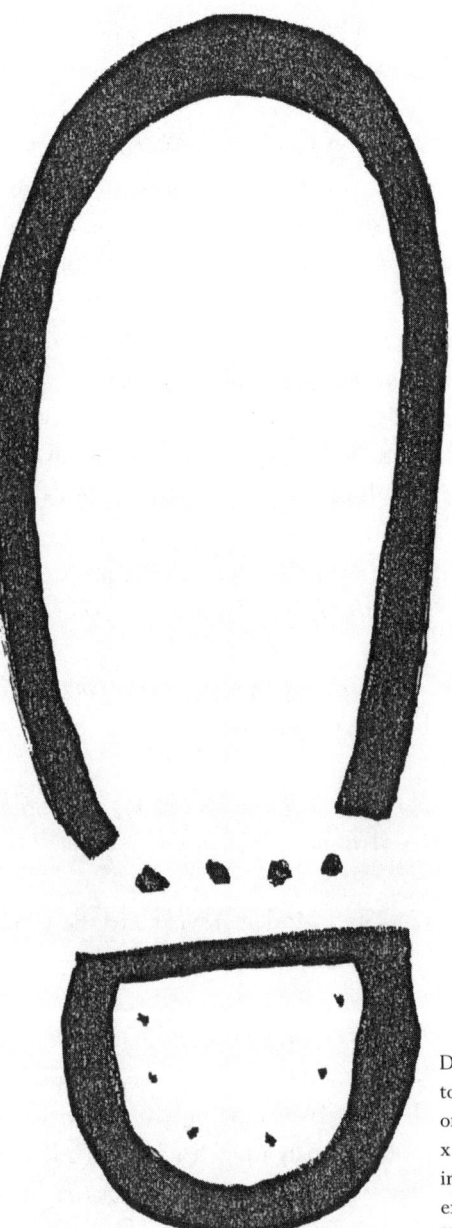

Figure 3

Draw this foot print to appropriate size on a piece of 8.5" x 11" paper for use in the posturing exercise (Part II, XI. b.)

XII. FILM #2: "Nurturing" using the entire film

    A. Facilitator's <u>Introductory Remarks</u>: "You will like this film. It shows fathers and mothers parenting. This is a reminder, or *how-to-do-it* flick."

        1. Sharing the burdens/responsibilities of parenting <u>can be</u> the sharing of the joys as well

        2. Watch <u>how</u> these parents deal with their children. After the showing, we will discuss points in the film of special interest to us

        3. Facilitators take a Census (by raising hands) of the age-groups of children in the Group. If some have adolescents, ask them to look for applications they can make from this film about preschool children

    B. Show the Film

    C. Discussion points to be used after the showing

        1. Feelings of "<u>the rejected stranger</u>"

            a.) What the Returnee may expect on homecoming

            b.) Possible jealous feelings about those who became "special people" during deployment absence

2. <u>Food mess on the floor</u> (perhaps just after parents held "field day")

   a.) What is the child "saying" by this behavior?

   b.) How did the mother handle it?

      (1) She understood why

      (2) Did not let it continue

      (3) Let the child "help"

3. <u>Hazards (kerosene lamp)</u>—if it had broken…

   a.) Whose fault would it have been?

   b.) Who probably would have gotten punished?

4. <u>Toy Cash Register</u>

   a.) Father had time for his daughter (instead of: "Come back during the commercial, kid.")

   b.) Film states: "This is how a child learns language, etc."

5. <u>Child at table grabs the cup</u>

   a.) Parents (Caregivers) show fairness

   b.) Parents are models of mature behavior

(1) Parenting is defined: "Getting the 'big people' to act bigger than the 'little people.'"

(2) Story: (Yelling at child) "Don't yell at your sister!"

6. <u>On the carpet with child and his book</u>

   a.) It is the obligation of the Parent to understand the Child, rather than the reverse

   b.) Small children do not have the obligation to understand adults. (Compare: Selective placement of items on market or commissary shelves so as to attract each age-group.)

7. Why buy so many toys (on deployment or cruise) to bring home to one's children?

   a.) [+] To tell them we love them

   b.) [-] A pay-off because we feel guilty for being away. (Why feel guilty for being away?)

   c.) Children overseas make/have simple toys, have fun. Enough?

D. Application of film discussion points to older children and teens [OMIT this Section if no parents of this age-group are among attendees]

1. (Messy food) -- What is the child "saying"? [*I want to be like you!*]

    a.) Tools left by child in the grass/rain

    b.) Records/tapes loaned to friends and become lost

    c.) Bedroom is a mess, clothes/shoes scattered, books/papers

2. (Child learns to clean up, pick up) – Learning responsibility

    a.) Home chores: mow lawn, carry out garbage, wash car, vacuum

    b.) Clean self: personal hygiene, pick up room, keep track of personal possessions

3. (Rejected Stranger) – Returning Parent feels left out

    a.) Older children are now building their own outside social world

    b.) To be <u>included</u>, <u>plan ahead</u>, make appointments with teens

4. (Hazards) – Whose fault would it be?

    a.) Driving with Learner's Permit – make time to teach and ride with a child under instruction – or give in to pleading and allow child to drive without sufficient experience

    b.) Dating allowed prior to discussions re: social/peer/sexual pressures young people experience

5. (Cash Register) – Time with child for bonding, setting aside work and social "obligations," golf, etc.

    a.) *Quality* time when parent cannot have *quantity* of time

    b.) One-on-one fun and discussions, outings, help with homework and projects, fishing together, Navy dependents' "Tiger cruises"

6. (Sitting on the rug with child)—Learning child's world

    a.) New world due to changes during the deployment-absence

    b.) Negotiate which activities can be shared, and when

7. (Grabs Cup) – Model for teaching behavior

   a.) Story: Parent tells child of intention to buy cheaper "Child's Ticket" for 12-year-old's birthday movie celebration, so they can buy ice cream with the savings

   b.) Child is proud of deserving an "Adult Ticket"

   c.) "What is parent teaching child?"
   Answer: To lie, cheat, steal

XIII. Feedback Discussion

   A. (Facilitator sits, facing Group): "What did you learn or were reminded of in this Seminar?"

   B. Facilitates Feedback Discussion [Note: It is usually brief. People are still processing the information.]

   C. Correct any <u>overly cautious</u> or anxious reactions. For example, reassure that Reunion *is not a problem*, but the more you know about it, the happier it can be!

XIV. Final Didactic and Review "Some things we have tried to <u>teach</u> or <u>remind you of</u> in this Seminar are…" [Briefly; No time to elaborate]

A. A family is like a mobile – it is *tied together* and *in balance*. But it is *living*, and therefore it is resistant to change, which is natural and to be expected

   1. The family mobile resists the leaving of the Service Member

   2. The family mobile confronts adjustments to the return

   3. Restoring the balance of the family mobile requires two four-letter words: *Time* and *Love*. Upon return home, allow for time, and express love

B. When you say (or think) "My Family," include yourself. Some of the adjustments to return (reunion) will be yours to make, also.

C. With the family, balance *Group Time* (all members together) with *Individual Time* (one-on-one with Spouse and also with each Child)

   1. Start with the "Honeymoon" (see above) – a weekend or a few days; Anticipate that the children may be jealous of your initial time away.

      a.) Offer child(ren) the opportunity of considering this additional time from them as a "homecoming gift" to you

      b.) "If it is better for us, your parents, it will be better for you."

c.) Promise, and keep it! Their special time with Returning Parent will come!

2. Have special event/day with each individual child; alternating with spouse

D. Be aware of children's tendency to *idolize* Returnee, and your tendency to *idolize* them

1. As the family comes together, <u>photographs come alive</u> revealing *real Humans*

a.) You will be revealed doing what parents do; feeling what parents feel. You will make mistakes, spank, may lose temper, apologize, etc.

b.) Sweet babies dirty diapers, cry/yell at night, get sick

c.) Kids whine: "But why do I have to…."

d.) Wives waken with curlers in their hair

2. Idolization is not all bad. Be aware of opportunities to teach family by your model of behavior and attitudes, and to be the object of their pride

E. Parenting is a *Skill*. You may be out-of-practice and need to play "catch-up," so <u>who can help and teach you</u> if you are willing?

1. Your Spouse

2. Your children themselves, so listen carefully to them

3. Books on parenting

4. Resource people: family therapists, chaplains/pastors, pediatricians, school teachers, mature relatives, etc.

5. Parenting seminars that may be held by Family Service Centers or Army Community Services

F. Closing Story (Facilitator makes it personal). My example: "The Joy and the Tragedy": Father and son were always close, but this was never overtly expressed until the father was 86, the son in 50's. Father was weak, embraces his adult son, saying: "I love you and I need you now." This was the first expression of our bonding.

1. Our culture's great lie: "Real men don't have feelings." This translates to: "Strong women don't have feelings."

2. Hug your loved ones, hold them. Tell them <u>how much you need them</u> and <u>how much you love them</u> NOW! Do not wait for years to do so.

G. Thank you and God bless you for coming. Now, go make it all happen!

SECTION B:

PRE-REUNION SEMINAR FOR SPOUSES PRIOR TO THE RETURN OF THOSE DEPLOYED

Title of presentation:
"IT'S ALL IN THE (Service Branch) FAMILY"

Note: This seminar is designed to be held in conjunction with its companion presented to Service Members at sea or in the field as they are preparing to return to their families. To expedite that seminar in a remote location, this phase of the program is to be held in advance of the one for Returnees. This is necessary so that reports of Spouses' "Fantasy/Reality Trip" will reach the Facilitators at the remote location in time to be used in the phase for the Returnees.

I. Introduction of Seminar and Facilitators

   A. Words of Welcome

   B. Purpose of the Seminar is to enrich the "return and reunion experience"

   C. Each Facilitator introduces the other Facilitator. Group urged to respond to each: "Hi, *First Name of Facilitator being introduced!*"

   D. Structure of the evening (or morning, afternoon)
      1. The importance of time discipline
      2. Participation of group members is encouraged

II. Creative Expectations

   A. Fantasy Trip: "Let's go on a Scottish Vacation" (Costs nothing); Close eyes…"Using your imagination or reports you have received, what is life like in the field (or on the ship)? Describe *in single words.*

      1. Facilitator #1 takes the answers, and agrees with Responder on single word descriptions (list answers)

      2. Facilitator #2 writes answers in Column #1 on Newsprint

         a.) Samples: dusty (or gray), hot, busy, no privacy, exciting (or boring), noise, no back-talk (withholding), no kids, anger, homesick, lonely, etc.

b.) *Then Facilitator asks for Positives:* travel, teamwork, hazardous duty/separation pay, professional growth, honor, friendships

3. Debrief by Facilitator: "Mind-reading can be mistaken! Therefore, we recommend that you check these things out with him/her on return to know if they are correct. We urge you to do this, and during this seminar we hope to assist you with good skills to do this, thus to <u>appreciate</u> your returnee."

B. Reality Trip: "What has life been like for you here at home?" Again use one- or two-word answers.

1. Facilitators use same process as before, but write this list on Column #2.

a.) Samples: work, lonely, responsible for everything, kids-kids-kids, being both mother and father, the unexpected, scared, insecurity (locks), busy, broke ($), car problems, tense, etc.

b.) *Then Facilitator asks for Positives:* Variety, self-sufficient, accomplishments, new job (or school), mail, personal growth, independent, learned to cope, etc.

2. Debrief by Facilitator:

   a.) "We want to share your one-word answers with your deployed spouse by message, just to give a hint as to what life has been like for you. It's important. Okay?"

   b.) "We suggest that you tell him/her more of this. You need to be <u>appreciated</u> as well. Your returnee cannot appreciate you unless he/she knows the *New You* better, as well as what you have accomplished. What you share/tell is up to you. However, we hope to improve your skills of telling/listening so as to make this easier for you."

III. Growth Index, Active Listening, Self-Appreciation

    A. *Provide a small notepad and pen/pencil.* Each participant is to list privately (using one- or two-word items on the pad) descriptive answers to the question: "Who were you when the Service Member left on deployment?" Then set this aside for future reference in this Seminar.

    B. Demonstration of Active Listening by 2 Facilitators. One Facilitator asks the attention of the other Facilitator; later in the conversation an important decision has to be made. *Note: A subject relevant to the group is prearranged.*

        1. <u>Bad example demonstration</u>: Facilitator acting as Teller asks for attention. Listener slouches, no eye contact, persists in changing the subject to matters of the Listener's own interest, is irrelevant.

            a.) At cut-off, Facilitator acting as Listener assesses frustration of observers

            b.) Listener then assesses anger of observers toward him/her (which gets Facilitator "out of role" with group).

            c.) Humorous comment: "Certainly nothing like this ever happens in the Army (Navy, Air Force, etc.)."

2. <u>Good example demonstration</u>: Teller asks for attention. Listener sits up and slightly forward, is animated in response

    a.) Facilitator acting as Teller explores situation, Listener uses good Active Listening skills as listed below

    b.) Teller faces a decision; Listener defines the decision, offers options. Listener does not make or favor the decision, but reflects assurance in the solution chosen by Teller. (E.g., "I am sure you will be pleased by your choice.")

3. Listener (now acting as Facilitator) *polls the Group* in an effort to get the following responses observed in the Listener's actions in the order given:

    a.) BODY LANGUAGE: Sits forward, animated, good eye contact, etc.

    b.) Picks up <u>first</u> on Teller's FEELINGS as he proceeds (explaining that feelings are the major communications link between two persons – like the wire between two telephones.) <u>Example for illustration</u>: Supervisor to angry Subordinate – "I can see that you are very uptight." This often begins to defuse a potentially explosive situation.

    c.) REPEATS BACK what Teller has said, keeps Teller on track, and reassures that the Listener has understood what has been told.

d.) REPHRASEs what has been told; similar to Repeating Back and serves the same purpose with slight variety.

e.) Uses the phrase: "DID I UNDERSTAND YOU TO SAY…?" to make possible corrections for both parties of the dialogue.

f.) Uses the phrase: "I HEAR YOU" to encourage Teller to advance.

g.) DEFINEs THE DECISION to be made by stating the options: "On the one hand (this)…, but on the other hand (that)…."

h.) In response to: "What should I do?" – "Well, what is YOUR PLAN?" or "What do you think is best?" By this, Listener encourages Teller to take responsibility.

i.) When a choice is made by Teller, reassures by saying: "YOU SEEM SATISFIED WITH YOUR DECISION."

C. <u>Didactic</u>: Previously prepared newsprint (with items in capital letters as above (in III. B. 3.) is now shown with the above items explained (giving credit to Group in places where these where items were observed. *This then continues with expanded explanation of the last two items:*

j.) NOT ADVICE GIVING

   1.) What is wrong with: "If I were you, I would…"? Anticipated Answer: "I'm not you." So this is an invasion of another's life. If the advice is <u>wrong</u>, it shifts the blame for the outcome away to another, and nothing is learned from this. If the advice is <u>right</u>, it lowers the self-esteem of the inquirer.

k.) NOT PASSIVE LISTENING – No feedback; the "Silent Listener"

   1.) Where is the information going? "Use Draino, or is the sewer pipe broken down below?"

   2.) Paranoia-producing Roll Play:

   <u>Teller</u>: "Let me tell you about Jane down the street." Derogatory remarks continue for awhile.

   <u>Listener</u>: Makes no responses, until finally she states: "She's my cousin, and I'm off to see her right now!" and walks out in anger.

D. Active Listening Practice

1. Form entire Group into dyads (groups of twos).

2. Set contract with Group:

    a.) First Listener is identified in each dyad (hold up hand)

    b.) Listener and Teller will switch on signal, <u>not before</u>

    c.) Time for the exercise is established; use Timer; halfway through call "time," and Listener and Teller change roles

    d.) Display list of Active Listening Skills on one newsprint (Capital letters in III. B. 3. and III. C.)

    e.) Urge participants to use Active Listening skills on the list (even if they seem exaggerated at first)

3. Task for the Practice is now assigned and displayed on the other newsprint "Describe yourself <u>now</u> (as the deployment is nearly over)." Listener has a small notepad to record items for the Teller entitled: "The *New Me*."

4. At the close of the exercise, each Teller is given her/his own list to hold.

E. Plenary Feedback from dyads (quickly conducted by Facilitator with the following questions):

1. Did you feel heard?

2. Was it easier to talk as the Teller?

3. Did you feel good about this exercise?

4. Facilitator comments (if appropriate): "The noise level was up, which indicates increased participation."

F. Each Participant is asked to look over her/his own "The *New Me*" list, and mark beside each self-description item a (+) for what they want to preserve, and a (-) for what is undesired and what they want to correct before their returnee arrives.

G. Each Participant introduces self to the Group, standing and sharing the (+) items on "The *New Me*" list. After each introduction, the Group is coached by the Facilitator to respond together, e.g., "Hi, Jane/John!")

H. Didactic by Facilitator: "Just like an exchange of gifts, when the reunion of a family after a deployment occurs, all family members will have achieved growth. In the "reunion process" of telling and listening and in learning to live together once again, the giving and receiving of "The *New Me's*" is the challenge and the joy of "Homecoming."

IV. FILM: "Nurturing"

A. Following brief introduction, show the film/video.

B. Discussion points to be used after the showing – optional, depending upon time, length of session, and apparent receptiveness of the attendees.

1. Regarding preschool and younger children: Use as outlined in Part II, Section A, XII. C.

2. Regarding older children and teenagers: Use as outlined in Part II, Section A, XII. D.

V. Homework is explained and urged:

A. When you go home - Write a thorough list of each child's present "Likes," "Dislikes," and "Current Activities"

B. When you go home - Write a thorough list of your own "Likes," "Dislikes," and "Current Activities"

C. Facilitator: "Then Make a copy of these lists. Mail the original to the Service Member in the field or onboard ship <u>right away</u>, keeping one in case it does not arrive prior to Homecoming"

VI. Refreshment Break and informal discussions, with Question & Answer time to follow, if appropriate. Individual problems that may not be of general interest may be referred for private consultations. Experience with this Seminar has demonstrated that more productivity is accomplished during break-time with spouses than with deployed troops. For this reason it is presented here as a final and open-ended activity. (Note: If the Break is held earlier in the process, it is not to exceed 10 minutes and be without a Q & A period. This is important in order to avoid any interruption of the planned sequence of the seminar. Informal discussions and Q & A can be positioned at the conclusion of the Seminar.)

About the DVD

FILMS ON DVD

Please see page 62 for further information about these films.

- *Ordinary People: A Film about Child Abuse.* For use with Part Two of this book. Our objective is to demonstrate the importance of the active listening skills taught in the seminar—<u>not</u> to suggest that child abuse is suspected. This film is part of the <u>Pre-Reunion Seminar for Returning Groups</u> (and is not recommended for the Spouses' Seminar).
- *Nurturing.* This video is essential for both the Seminar For Returning Groups (Section A), and the Seminar For Spouses (Section B).

PRINTABLE DOCUMENTS

All documents in 8.5" x 11" pdf format

- Seminar For Returning Groups (Section A).
- Seminar For Spouses (Section B).
- Reunion Ideas to Take Home for Returning Personnel
- Reunion Ideas to Take Home for Spouses

Please note: The two Films may be shown on any DVD player. However, to access the Films and the Printable Documents that are to be used for the Pre-Reunion Seminars using a computer, a DVD ROM Drive and Adobe Reader are required. [If Adobe Reader is needed, go to www.adobe.com for free download of the Reader.] When the DVD is inserted in the computer DVD ROM Drive, a menu will appear showing both films. To access the Printable Documents; double-click on "My Computer" on the Desk Top to reveal the DVD ROM icon. Right-click on the DVD ROM icon and select "Explore," then left-click on "Explore" to view the four pdf "Printable Resources" files.